Focus on Zimbabwe

FOCUS ON ZIMBABWE

ALFRED J. CARTAGE
EDITOR

Nova Science Publishers, Inc.
New York

LIBRARY OF CONGRESS CATALOGING-IN-PUBLICATION DATA

ISBN: 978-1-60692-186-9

Published by Nova Science Publishers, Inc. ; New York

CONTENTS

PREFACE

Zimbabwe's prospects appeared promising in 1980, as it gained independence after a long liberation war. The country exhibited steady economic growth, enabling the new government to provide free education and widespread access to health care. Challenges grew in the 1990s, however. Rising inflation and unemployment bred discontent, as evidenced by regular student and labor protests, and led in 1999 to the formation of the opposition Movement for Democratic Change (MDC). The new party surprised many with its initial success, campaigning against a 2000 referendum that would have legalized the president's continued rule, made government officials immune from prosecution, and allowed the uncompensated seizure of white-owned land for redistribution to black farmers. The referendum failed, and the MDC won nearly half the seats in the 2000 parliamentary election. The ruling party has since taken numerous, often undemocratic actions to bolster its power, including an aggressive land redistribution policy.

President Robert Mugabe's government is seen as autocratic and repressive by its critics, and its human rights record is poor. The regime suppresses freedom of speech and assembly, and many contend that the government restricts access to food, already scarce, in opposition areas. The MDC, divided over how to respond, split into two factions in 2005, hampering its ability to challenge the ruling party. Mugabe has repeatedly extended his rule and has been chosen by his party to stand as its presidential candidate again in the upcoming March 29, 2008 elections. A behind the- scenes power struggle within his party adds to questions regarding the country's future; former finance minister and ex-ruling party member Simba Makoni will stand against Mugabe, and opposition leader Morgan Tsvangirai, in the presidential race.

Zimbabwe's economic output has decreased 40% since 1998, official inflation rose above 8,000% in 2007, and unemployment is estimated at more than

80%. A widely criticized urban cleanup program in 2005 resulted in the demolition of thousands of homes and businesses in poor urban areas, seen by the government as a base of MDC support. The adult HIV infection rate of 20% has contributed to a sharp drop in life expectancy, and more than a third of the population is expected to require food aid in 2008. Deteriorating conditions in the country have led many to emigrate to neighboring countries, creating a substantial burden on the region.

Chapter 1 - President Mugabe has enjoyed considerable popularity in Africa as a former liberation leader. However, some African leaders have come to see his conduct as damaging to the continent and are urging democratic reforms. South Africa has pursued "quiet diplomacy" aimed at resolving the problems in Zimbabwe through dialogue between the government and opposition, but many view this policy as ineffective. Following controversial elections in 2000 and citing abuses of human rights and the rule of law, the United States and other former allies of the government have become vocal critics. The U.S. Secretary of State has labeled Zimbabwe an "outpost of tyranny," and the United States has enforced targeted sanctions against top Zimbabwe officials and associates since 2002. This report includes recent developments and reactions from the international community, including those of the United States. This report will be updated as events warrant.

Chapter 2 - On March 29, 2008, Zimbabwe held presidential, parliamentary and local elections. More than a month later, the country's political future remains uncertain. For the first time since independence, the ruling party has lost its majority in the National Assembly. After a month of rising tensions, the results of the presidential race were belatedly announced on May 2. They indicated that opposition leader Morgan Tsvangirai had received more votes than the incumbent, President Robert Mugabe, but had failed to garner the 50 percent needed to avoid a runoff.

Reports of violence and political repression have increased significantly since the elections, which were held amidst a deepening economic crisis in the Southern African country. Zimbabwe's gross domestic product (GDP) has decreased over 40 percent in the last decade, the inflation rate is estimated at over 165,000 percent, and unemployment is higher than 80 percent. The adult HIV infection rate of 20 percent has contributed to a sharp drop in life expectancy, and more than a third of the population is expected to require food aid in 2008. Deteriorating conditions in the country have led many Zimbabweans to emigrate to neighboring countries, creating a substantial burden on the region. In South Africa, Zimbabwean immigrants and others have recently been the target of xenophobic attacks.

President Mugabe's government is seen as autocratic and repressive by its critics, and its human rights record is poor. The regime has suppressed freedom of speech and assembly, and many contend that it restricts access to food, already scarce, in opposition areas. Many regional and international observers suggest the presidential runoff, which the government has postponed until June 27, should not be held amidst the current level of political violence. The U.S. Secretary of State has labeled Zimbabwe an "outpost of tyranny," and other Administration officials have accused the ruling party of rigging the election and orchestrating the current violence. The United States has enforced targeted sanctions against top Zimbabwe officials and associates since 2002. Congress has expressed its opposition to the government's undemocratic policies in the Zimbabwe Democracy and Economic Recovery Act of 200 1(P.L. 107-99) and other subsequent legislation, including H.Con.Res. 100, S.Con.Res. 25, S. 1500, S.Res. 533, and H.Res. 1230 during the 1 10th Congress. For more background, see CRS Report RL32723, *Zimbabwe*.

In: Focus on Zimbabwe
Editor: Alfred J. Cartage, pp. 1-53

ISBN: 978-1-60692-186-9

Chapter 1

ZIMBABWE*

Lauren Ploch
Analyst in African Affairs
Foreign Affairs, Defense, and Trade Division

ABSTRACT

Zimbabwe's prospects appeared promising in 1980, as it gained independence after a long liberation war. The country exhibited steady economic growth, enabling the new government to provide free education and widespread access to health care. Challenges grew in the 1990s, however. Rising inflation and unemployment bred discontent, as evidenced by regular student and labor protests, and led in 1999 to the formation of the opposition Movement for Democratic Change (MDC). The new party surprised many with its initial success, campaigning against a 2000 referendum that would have legalized the president's continued rule, made government officials immune from prosecution, and allowed the uncompensated seizure of white-owned land for redistribution to black farmers. The referendum failed, and the MDC won nearly half the seats in the 2000 parliamentary election. The ruling party has since taken numerous, often undemocratic actions to bolster its power, including an aggressive land redistribution policy.

President Robert Mugabe' s government is seen as autocratic and repressive by its critics, and its human rights record is poor. The regime suppresses freedom of speech and assembly, and many contend that the government restricts access to food, already scarce, in opposition areas. The MDC,

---

* Excerpted from CRS Report RL32723, dated March 25, 2008.

divided over how to respond, split into two factions in 2005, hampering its ability to challenge the ruling party. Mugabe has repeatedly extended his rule and has been chosen by his party to stand as its presidential candidate again in the upcoming March 29, 2008 elections. A behindthe-scenes power struggle within his party adds to questions regarding the country's future; former finance minister and ex-ruling party member Simba Makoni will stand against Mugabe, and opposition leader Morgan Tsvangirai, in the presidential race.

Zimbabwe's economic output has decreased 40% since 1998, official inflation rose above 8,000% in 2007, and unemployment is estimated at more than 80%. A widely criticized urban cleanup program in 2005 resulted in the demolition of thousands of homes and businesses in poor urban areas, seen by the government as a base of MDC support. The adult HIV infection rate of 20% has contributed to a sharp drop in life expectancy, and more than a third of the population is expected to require food aid in 2008. Deteriorating conditions in the country have led many to emigrate to neighboring countries, creating a substantial burden on the region.

President Mugabe has enjoyed considerable popularity in Africa as a former liberation leader. However, some African leaders have come to see his conduct as damaging to the continent and are urging democratic reforms. South Africa has pursued "quiet diplomacy" aimed at resolving the problems in Zimbabwe through dialogue between the government and opposition, but many view this policy as ineffective. Following controversial elections in 2000 and citing abuses of human rights and the rule of law, the United States and other former allies of the government have become vocal critics. The U.S. Secretary of State has labeled Zimbabwe an "outpost of tyranny," and the United States has enforced targeted sanctions against top Zimbabwe officials and associates since 2002. This report includes recent developments and reactions from the international community, including those of the United States. This report will be updated as events warrant.

Recent Developments

With official inflation[1] rising above 8,000% in late 2007, Zimbabwe's economy continues to collapse, and the outlook for its people remains grave. Following the March 2007 assault by police on government critics, South African President Thabo Mbeki began a mediation effort between the government of Zimbabwe and the opposition. The talks resulted in some changes to laws regarded by many as repressive leading up to the country's next elections, expected to occur on March 29, 2008. Human rights activists argue that the changes are cosmetic and that the talks have failed to create a level playing field prior to the elections.[2]

March 2007 Arrests

Zimbabwe received international media attention for the March 11, 2007, crackdown on opposition and civil society activists, during which one opposition supporter was shot and killed by police (see "Opposition Defiance" section below). Opposition leader Morgan Tsvangirai and several others allegedly received severe beatings by police following their arrest. Tsvangirai and others were accused of violating a three-month ban on public protests instated by the Zimbabwean government in mid-February. They were released into the custody of their lawyers days after the arrest. Two opposition officials who were arrested were later allowed to go to South Africa to receive medical treatment for their injuries. According to media reports, police initially refused to allow their departure, and another opposition official, Nelson Chamisa, was allegedly beaten at the airport when he tried to leave. Tsvangirai was detained again, along with other party members, for several hours on March 28 in a police raid on the opposition headquarters.

South African Mediation

International criticism of the situation in Zimbabwe grew after the arrests, even among former allies on the continent. In one of the most critical statements from African leaders, Zambia's President Levy Mwanawasa compared the country to "a sinking Titanic whose passengers are jumping out to save their lives."[3] One of South Africa's Deputy Foreign Ministers told the South African parliament, "The South African government wishes to express its concern, disappointment, and disapproval of the measures undertaken by the security forces in dealing with the political protests," blaming the current situation on an "absence of open political dialogue."[4] Southern African Development Community (SADC) leaders convened an emergency summit on March 28, 2007.

Given the strong statements made by some southern African leaders, many observers expected the SADC heads of state to increase pressure on Mugabe to make reforms. Reports suggest that in private the leaders may have been tough on the Zimbabwean president, who was in attendance, but their public response was deemed disappointing by human rights activists and critics of the regime.[5] During the summit, the SADC leaders resolved to promote dialogue within the country, at the same time suggesting that western countries should drop their sanctions against the Mugabe government and that Britain should provide funding to assist in land reform efforts. South African President Thabo Mbeki was appointed to mediate between the Zimbabwean government and the opposition. Mbeki has insisted he is not in favor of regime change and has pushed instead for democratic elections, saying "you might question whether these elections are genuinely free and fair ... but we have to get the Zimbabweans talking so we do have elections that are free and fair."[6] Talks between the Mugabe Administration and the MDC factions began in Pretoria in June 2007.

According to human rights activists and the U.S. Department of State, political violence against opposition leaders and supporters continued in spite of the negotiations.[7] The Mugabe Administration accused the opposition of being responsible for a series of bombings targeting shops, trains, and police stations, although some observers suggest the attacks were an attempt to frame the MDC.[8] Harassment of university students by police also reportedly increased. On November 22, 2007, 22 members of the National Constitutional Assembly, a pro-democracy civil society organization, reportedly sustained severe beatings during a peaceful protest set to coincide with a visit by President Mbeki to Harare.[9]

Although the South Africa negotiations resulted in several agreements between the parties, leading to the amendment of some laws seen to restrict press freedom and political activity, the talks were abandoned after Mugabe announced that elections would be held on March 29, 2008. Despite President Mbeki's report to SADC leaders that his mediation had achieved "commendable achievements," Morgan Tsvangirai announced in February 2008 that "nothing has changed. ..changes in the law, negotiated by President Mbeki, have not changed the behavior of the dictatorship."[10]

March 2008 Elections

The two factions of the main opposition party, the Movement for Democratic Change (MDC), which split in 2005, remain divided. Despite rumors of dissatisfaction with Mugabe' s continued rule from within his own party, the party's central committee voted in March 2007 to nominate Mugabe to be the party's candidate in the next elections. The committee also supported a resolution to hold all elections (presidential, parliamentary, and local council) at the same time, in March 2008, and to reduce the terms for all public offices from six to five years. In addition, they voted back efforts to increase the number of parliamentarians from 150 to 210 and the number of senators from 66 to 84.[11] Critics contend that these proposals are an attempt to manipulate the electoral process through gerrymandering, with the new constituencies created in rural areas where the ruling party has stronger support.[12] ZANU-PF also proposed to allow the parliament to select a new president if the sitting president resigns, is incapacitated, or dies in office.[13] Analysts suggest that Mugabe may not intend to serve an entire term if re-elected, instead planning to resign mid-term and use parliament to hand-pick his successor.[14]

The proposals were included in a controversial Constitutional Amendment Bill, which, to the surprise of many observers, was passed by the parliament in September 2007 with the support of MDC MPs. The final version of the legislation, did, however, include some changes seen as concessions to the opposition, and reports suggest that the MDC's support of the legislation came as a result of progress in the negotiations in South Africa.

In February 2008, then-ZANU-PF senior member Simba Makoni announced his intention to run against President Mugabe in the upcoming elections. He was subsequently expelled from the party and is running as an independent, although he is rumored to have the support of several unnamed senior party officials. Makoni, 57, served as Finance Minister from 2000 to 2002 and was reportedly dismissed after criticizing the administration's economic policies. Makoni also previously served as the executive secretary of SADC. Opposition leader Tsvangirai has dismissed Makoni as "old wine in a new bottle," but rival MDC leader Arthur Mutambara has withdrawn as a presidential candidate and expressed his support for Makoni.

The Zimbabwean government has reportedly invited election observers from 47 countries and regional organizations, including SADC, although it is allegedly barring observers from countries considered to be critical of its policies.[15] CNN and other western media organizations and journalists have also reportedly been denied permission to cover the elections.[16] The National Constitutional Assembly, which has criticized the government for excluding some observers, suggests that the ruling party has manipulated state resources for campaign purposes and redrawn constituencies to ensure its continued hold on power. The Zimbabwe Election Support Network (ZESN), a domestic civil society group, suggests that there are not enough polling stations in urban areas, where the opposition is believed to have its strongest support, and the Network has urged the electoral commission to increase the number of stations in Harare and Bulawayo provinces.[17] In the weeks preceding the election, President Mugabe has announced a significant salary increase for civil servants and has signed into law the Indigenisation and Economic Empowerment Bill, which requires foreign-owned firms to transfer 51% of their shares to domestic investors.

BACKGROUND[18]

After years of economic sanctions by the international community and a decades-long civil war that resulted in more than 30,000 dead, the white minority rule government of Southern Rhodesia concluded a series of agreements with the black majority in 1979 that resulted in the establishment of the government of the Republic of Zimbabwe. Among the greatest challenges facing the new government was the demand by the majority for greater equity in land distribution.[19] At independence, the white minority, who composed less than 5% of the population, owned the vast majority of arable land. Many observers considered the country's white-owned commercial farms crucial to the country's economy, although there was a general recognition that land reform was necessary. Britain initially funded a "willing buyer, willing seller" program to redistribute commercial farmland, offering compensation to white farmers amenable to leaving their lands.

Dissatisfaction with the pace of land reform grew and led in the 1990s to spontaneous and often violent farm invasions. At the same time, the country's labor movement and a segment of its urban middle class were becoming increasingly critical of the government's economic performance. Facing rising political and economic challenges, the government of Zimbabwe began to implement aggressive land expropriation policies, leading Britain and other donors to begin withdrawing financial support for resettlement.

In 2000, the government held a referendum to approve changes to the constitution that would allow land seizures without compensation, a responsibility that in its view lay with Britain. The referendum was rejected by 55% of voters and was seen as a victory for a new opposition party, the Movement for Democratic Change (MDC). Within days of the vote war veterans and ruling party supporters moved onto an estimated 1,000 white-owned farms, and, months later, the President invoked emergency powers to take land without compensation. During this time there were numerous attacks against white farmers and their employees, as well as against supporters of the MDC; more than 30 people were killed.

Since then, the country's problems have deepened. Substantial political violence and human rights violations accompanied parliamentary elections in 2000 and 2005 and the presidential election in 2002. There are continuing reports of human rights abuses and of food being used as a political weapon. Zimbabwe's political difficulties have been accompanied by a sharp decline in living standards, with more than 80% of the population living on less than $2 per day.[20] Once touted as a potential "breadbasket of Africa," much of Zimbabwe's population is now dependent on food aid. More than 20% of adults in Zimbabwe are infected by the HIV/AIDS virus, and life expectancy fell from an estimated 56 years in 1990 to 39.5 in 2007.[21] In fact, according to the World Health Organization (WHO), the life expectancy for Zimbabwean women is just 34, the lowest in the world. Foreign Policy magazine has ranked Zimbabwe fourth in its index of failed states.[22]

Observers are concerned that the difficulties confronting Zimbabwe are affecting neighboring countries and deterring investors from the region.

Zimbabwe at a Glance

Population: 12.3 million
Approximate size: Slightly larger than Montana
Population growth rate: 0.595%
Life expectancy at birth: 39.5 years
Ethnic groups: African 98% (Shona 82%, Ndebele 14%, other 2%), Mixed and Asian 1%, White less than 1%
Languages: English (official), Shona, Sindebele and a number of tribal dialects. **Literacy:** *Total Population:* 90.7%; *Male:* 94.2%; *Female:* 87.2%
GDP real growth rate: -4.4%
GNI Per Capita (Atlas Method): $350
HIV Infection Rate: 20.1% (adults, aged 15-49)
Unemployment: 80%
Sources: CIA World Factbook; Economist Intelligence Unit; UNAIDS

Political Situation

Zimbabwe has been ruled since independence by the Zimbabwe African National Union-Patriotic Front (ZANU-PF), which has come under increasing scrutiny from human rights activists, both at home and abroad. Critics cite high levels of corruption, political violence, and strictly enforced laws restricting basic freedoms. The government contends its detractors have engaged in a "propaganda war" backed by Britain and the United States, using democracy and human rights as a cover to push for regime change.[23] Many domestic and international observers have judged elections since 2000 to be "far from free and fair." The country's main opposition party, the Movement for Democratic Change (MDC), split over tactical issues in 2005, and although there have been attempts at reconciliation, the party remains divided. The ruling party has also suffered internal competition, and some observers suggest opposition to President Mugabe himself has grown within the party. The timing of a political transition in Zimbabwe, and the means by which it will occur, cannot be predicted, but with Mugabe in his 80s, it appears inevitable.

Parliamentary Elections 2005

Zimbabwe held its most recent legislative elections in 2005. The elections, like those before them in 2000 and 2002, were controversial, with the opposition disputing the results and alleging government efforts to deny a fair race. ZANU-PF retained control of the 150-member parliament, taking 108 seats (of these, 30 are appointed by the President rather than elected). The opposition MDC won 41 seats, and one seat went to an independent.[24]

The MDC's representation in parliament has declined since 2000, when it won 57 seats in its first elections. Some observers argue that the MDC did not do as well in the 2005 election because it delayed a decision to participate until December 2004, leaving little time to campaign. Violence against MDC voters in past elections, and the alleged use of food distributions by the ruling party to secure votes, and a general climate of intimidation may have also discouraged MDC support. Government supporters suggest voters simply lost faith in MDC promises.

Opposition access to the state-run media was severely limited, according to Reporters Without Borders, a Paris-based organization that supports press freedom.[25] The MDC was rarely covered on television or in the *Herald*, the government-controlled newspaper, and the stories that did appear were typically disparaging.

Election-Related Violence

Although most observers agree that the level of political violence surrounding the 2005 elections was significantly less than that which preceded the 2000 and 2002 elections, many argue the election was not "free and fair," and that there were some incidents of violence. Critics suggest that state harassment of civil society and the political opposition, combined with limitations on press and other political freedoms, left little need for violent repression. Nevertheless, the Zimbabwe Human Rights NGO Forum, a coalition of 17 human rights organizations, reported more than 300 assaults in the pre- election period.[26]

Charges of Election Rigging

Many analysts argue that the Zimbabwean political system is undemocratic because elections are administered by institutions and under laws that many consider biased in favor of the ruling party. In response to democratic protocols established by the Southern African Development Community (SADC), the government passed the Zimbabwe Electoral Commission (ZEC) Act and the Electoral Act prior to the 2005 elections. However, the new "independent" ZEC, appointed by the president, was only established two months before the election, leaving many of the preparations to the old Electoral Commission, which many considered discredited by its past performance. According to the U.S.-based democracy advocacy group Freedom House, "despite some improvements, the Electoral Act granted the ZEC powers to employ security forces, retained biased residency requirements for voters, denied most expatriates the right to vote, and created an Electoral Court staffed by a deeply compromised judiciary."[27]

The Mugabe government has employed other legal tactics seen by critics as designed to intimidate the opposition and produce a political landscape favorable to ZANU-PF. The 2004 gerrymandering of constituencies, which the government attributed to population shifts arising from its land reform program, resulted in the redistricting of three urban seats held by the MDC into three new rural constituencies, which ZANU-PF candidates won in 2005. The International Council of Barristers and Advocates described extensive efforts by ZANU-PF to gain control over the legal system in a 2004 report, suggesting the ruling party has interfered in judicial appointments and forced the removal of impartial judges "through a combination of psychological and physical intimidation and threats of violence."[28]

The MDC has challenged the results of 16 races in court, claiming that the election was rigged. Their allegations focus on several largely rural districts in which the ZEC announced voter turnout totals before the vote results were reported. Once the results came in, the ZANU-PF candidate won in each case, but the vote for the two candidates added together exceeded the initial ZEC-reported turnout total. This created a suspicion that additional votes had been given to the ZANU-PF candidates during the tabulation phase to prevent MDC victories. The ZEC eventually halted the release of turnout totals, so it is not known if there were similar discrepancies in other districts. According to the ZEC, they had initially released early totals coming in to provide an indication of voter turnout, and the discrepancies between those initial figures and the final tallies were due to poor communications from rural areas. Other opposition allegations focus on large numbers of voters were reportedly turned away by poll officials for alleged registration problems, which seem to have been more common in contested areas than in districts regarded as safe for ZANU-PF.

Although none of the 2005 results have been overturned, a 2006 Zimbabwean supreme court decision gave the opposition further legal recourse. Against the arguments of the chief justice, the attorney-general, and the justice minister, the court ruled that the judicial appointment of commissioners to the electoral court was unconstitutional and violated the principle of separation of powers.[29]

Election Observers

Many domestic election observers, such as the Zimbabwe Lawyers for Human Rights (ZLHR) and the Zimbabwe Election Support Network (ZESN), were critical of the elections. During the pre-election period, they cited a lack of transparency surrounding voter registration as a "significant and serious threat to the overall credibility of the electoral process." Their reports cited no incidents of overt political violence, but noted the pre-election period was marked by intimidation, "politicization of food distribution," and a lack of media access by the opposition. The observers contended they were restricted access to the vote counting process at many polling stations, and that in some cases the total voter tally did not coincide with the total number of votes cast for the candidates.[30] Both groups reported the use of POSA, MOA, and AIPPA throughout the election period against opposition supporters. The ZLHR report concluded, "Zimbabwean authorities have failed, on most accounts, to ensure a free and fair electoral process."[31]

The Mugabe regime placed limits on foreign observers for the election. No U.S. observers were invited, and Russia was the only European country asked to send a team. Leading the Southern African Development Community (SADC) delegation, South African Deputy President Mlambo-Ngcuka congratulated Zimbabwe on "the holding of a peaceful, credible, well managed and transparent election. The people of Zimbabwe have expressed their will in an impressively instructive manner that will go a long way in contributing to the consolidation of democracy and political stability not only in Zimbabwe, but also in the region as a whole."[32] The head of South Africa's parliamentary observer mission was quoted saying that the delegation had "unanimously agreed that the elections were credible, legitimate, free and fair."[33] Both statements received substantial criticism in the international press. The SADC Parliamentary Forum, which consists of legislators from the region and had issued a report critical of the 2002 election, was not invited to observe the vote.

Western governments condemned the elections. Based on reports from domestic observers and U.S. Embassy staff who were allowed to observe the election, U.S. Secretary of State Condoleezza Rice issued the following statement:

> Although the campaign and election day itself was generally peaceful, the election process was not free and fair. The electoral playing field was heavily tilted in the government's favor. The independent press was muzzled; freedom of assembly was constrained; food was used as a weapon to sway hungry voters; and millions of Zimbabweans who have been forced by the nation's economic collapse to emigrate were disenfranchised.[34]

U.N. Secretary-General Kofi Annan commended the election's lack of violence but noted concern that "the electoral process has not countered the sense of disadvantage felt by opposition political parties who consider the conditions were unfair."[35]

Restrictions on Political Freedoms

Legislative actions in the ZANU-PF-dominated parliament have raised concerns about human rights in Zimbabwe. Laws that critics contend are used to quiet dissent and influence political developments include the following:

- *The Access to Information and Protection of Privacy Act (AIPPA).* This 2002 Act requires that all media services be licensed, and that all journalists, including foreign correspondents, be officially accredited. The government, citing AIPPA, closed *The Daily News*, the only remaining independent daily, in 2003. In 2005, three Zimbabwean correspondents for the Associated Press, Bloomberg News, and the *Times* of London, fled Zimbabwe after police raided their office. The Media Institute of Southern Africa (MISA) has stated that AIPPA is "one of the most effective legal instruments of state control over the media and civil society communication anywhere in the world."[36] The government counters that AIPPA encourages responsible journalism.
- *The Public Order and Security Act (POSA), the Criminal Law (Codification and Reform) Act ("Criminal Law Code"), and the Miscellaneous Offences Act (MOA).* POSA, also enacted in 2002, prohibits statements deemed to be "abusive, indecent, obscene, or false" about the president or considered to "undermin(e) public confidence" in the security forces, and prohibits false statements prejudicial to the state.[37] The measure has been used in the arrest of thousands of political opponents and in police action to break up public meetings and demonstrations. Zimbabweans overheard criticizing the President in a public place have also been jailed. The MOA criminalized "conduct likely to cause a breach of the peace," and was often used with POSA against activists. Police and "persons assisting the police" may use "all necessary force" to stop unlawful gatherings.[38] In 2006 many offences under POSA and MOA were transferred to the new Criminal Law Code.
- *Non-Governmental Organizations (NGO) Bill and the Private Voluntary Organizations (PVO) Act.* The controversial NGO Bill, pushed through parliament in 2004 despite objections to its constitutionality, has not been signed into law by the President, although concerns remain

> about its future. The bill would have prohibited foreign NGOs from operating in Zimbabwe if their principal objectives include "issues of governance," which in turn include "the promotion and protection of human rights."[39] Domestic NGOs would have been prohibited from accepting foreign funds for activities involving issues of governance. Instead, the government uses the PVO Act, enacted in 2002. NGOs are required to register with the government, and a "probe team" of intelligence officers has wide powers to investigate groups and demand documents related to activities and funding. The African Commission on Human and Peoples' Rights has recommended that it be repealed.

The opposition has had limited success in preventing the ruling party from passing other legislation that it contends would restrict freedoms. The Interception of Communications Bill, which would allow the government to monitor all Internet, email, and telephone communications for threats to national security, was stalled by the Parliamentary Legal Committee (chaired by an MDC MP), but was later revised and approved in June 2007. Critics suggest the revisions are cosmetic.

In the 2005 elections ZANU-PF won over two-thirds of the seats in the House of Assembly, giving the party the power to amend the constitution. Since then, the parliament has passed several controversial constitutional amendments which some analysts contend breach international human rights standards. The 2005 Constitution of Zimbabwe Amendment Act (No.17) allows the government to limit the right to freedom of movement when it is in "the public interest" or in "the economic interests of the State" and restricts the right to leave Zimbabwe. Several journalists, MDC officials, and union leaders have had their passports revoked under the act; the government has charged that they planned to lobby abroad for sanctions or military intervention against the country.[40] The act also prevents land owners from challenging the acquisition of agricultural land by the state. It paved the way for the passage of Gazetted Land (Consequential Provisions) Act in late 2006, making it illegal for former farm owners to occupy nationalized land and allowing the government to evict farmers and resettle the land without compensation. The constitutional amendment also revived the upper house of the parliament, the Senate, which was abolished in 1989.

The South Africa-led SADC negotiations led in January 2008 to amendments to both AIPPA and POSA. Critics suggest the amendments do not adequately address human rights concerns and are not being implemented.[41] They cite, for example, a January 2008 MDC "freedom march" that was blocked by police despite prior notification of the event, in accordance with the changes to POSA. Supporters who defied a police ban were reportedly tear-gassed and beaten with batons. The Media Institute of Southern Africa has dismissed the amendments to AIPPA as "dwelling ... on inconsequential issues which will not advance basic freedoms."[42]

2005 Senate Elections

Elections to the new 66-seat Senate were held in September 2005, and were marked by record low voter turnout. Of 26 MDC candidates who ran, seven were elected; ZANU-PF gained the overwhelming majority of seats. Observers suggest one of the reasons for the low turnout may have been a lack of solidarity on the part of the opposition, which split prior to the election over whether to boycott the vote.

Presidential Succession

In view of President Mugabe' s advanced age, presidential succession a matter of intense interest to analysts. Some observers worry that if elections do not lead to a democratic transfer of power in the upcoming elections, Zimbabwe could experience a violent succession struggle or a possible military coup. Under the constitution, the president may designate one of the country's two vice presidents to serve as acting president until the next election, should he leave office, but Mugabe has not done so. One of the vice presidential posts was vacant prior to the 2004 ZANU-PF party conference, setting off a power struggle that transformed the political scene by revealing internal party divisions. Despite his age, President Mugabe is reportedly in good health and in no rush to relinquish his post. Many observers suggest he has used the country's anti-corruption authority to check the political ambitions of his party members. Mugabe endorsed a 2007 proposal to extend the next presidential elections to 2010, but it was defeated by the ruling party's central committee. He has been nominated by his party as its presidential candidate in the upcoming elections.

Who Will Succeed Mugabe?

Prior to ZANU-PF' s December 2004 party conference, Emmerson Mnangagwa, then speaker of the parliament and a political veteran long touted as Mugabe' s heir, campaigned actively for the position of ZANU-PF's second vice president. His selection to that position would likely have assured his appointment as national vice president, but Mnangagwa was caught off guard when Mugabe decided that the country should have a woman in the post. Mugabe' s choice for the position, Joice Mujuru, was inevitably elected, and she was sworn into office as Zimbabwe's second vice president. Mujuru, a veteran of the liberation war and a women's movement leader, had been serving as Minister of Water Resources and Infrastructure.

The outcome of any succession struggle will likely be affected by the country's ethnic and clan divisions. Mugabe and many key party and clan officials are from the Zezuru clan of the Shona people, who are dominant in a wide area encircling Harare, the country's capital. One of Mugabe' s closest advisors, regarded as a king-maker, is retired General Solomon "Rex" Mujuru, a Zezuru and husband of Joice Mujuru. Mnangagwa was seen as a representative of the large Karanga clan, which reportedly felt that its turn to control the reins of power had come. Mnangagwa' s viability as a presidential contender was hampered by accusations that he led the purge of alleged regime opponents in provinces of Matabeleland in the 1980s, which is believed to have resulted in the deaths of 20,000 Ndebele civilians. The events of the 1980s help to explain why Bulawayo has long been regarded as a center of opposition to the government, although Mugabe has sought to gain support in the region by elevating a number of Ndebele to party and government posts.

In any event, Mnangagwa' s power has been reduced, as has that of a number of his backers, including the former minister of information, Jonathan Moyo. Moyo was fired in early 2005 for his sharp-tongued defenses of the regime and for picking spats with other ZANU-PF leaders. He deeply angered Mugabe by convening an unsanctioned meeting of Mnangagwa supporters before the party convention, allegedly to strategize on ways of derailing the Mujuru candidacy. Moyo left the party and ran as an independent in 2005.

According to reports, neither the Mnangagwa nor Mujuru camps supported Mugabe' s proposed term extension. Solomon Mujuru has been vocal in his disapproval and is rumored to have been pivotal in blocking the proposal at the party's national conference. Some have suggested that Mujuru is covertly backing another ZANU-PF official, Simba Makoni, over his wife as a potential successor to Mugabe. Makoni, a technocrat, has been considered by some analysts to be a compromise candidate, untainted by the corruption scandals that have plagued others. Mugabe' s own choice for his successor is unknown, but many suggest he might back Reserve Bank Chairman Gideon Gono. Regardless, the party's decision to choose Mugabe as its candidate for the 2008 elections, and Makoni's decision to run against him as an independent candidate, suggests the succession speculation will continue for the foreseeable future.

The Movement for Democratic Change (MDC)

Origins of the MDC

The MDC party rose from the Zimbabwe labor movement. As poverty deepened in Zimbabwe in the late 1990s, and allegations of corruption against regime leaders became more frequent, the Zimbabwe Congress of Trade Unions (ZCTU) organized a number of strikes and protests. In September 1999, the MDC was formed on this trade union base with support from many in Zimbabwe's churches and in urban areas. In February 2000, MDC members elected the ZCTU secretary general, Morgan Tsvangirai (CHANG-gerai), born in 1952, as MDC president, and union president Gibson Sibanda as MDC vice president.

The MDC proved formidable in the 2000 referendum and in the 2000 parliamentary election; some contend their success may have prompted a range of repressive actions against the party and its supporters. Among the retaliatory measures alleged, several leaders of the MDC, including Tsvangirai himself, were arrested and charged with treason two weeks before the MDC leader ran against Mugabe in the 2002 presidential elections.

Treason Charges

On October 15, 2004, Tsvangirai was acquitted of a treason charge based on a video recorded in Canada, which the government claimed showed him calling for the "elimination" of Mugabe. The verdict surprised many observers in view of the regime's perceived influence over the courts. The judge stated that the evidence had been unconvincing, with the witnesses produced by the state "suspect" and the video unreliable. The government can appeal the verdict, and Tsvangirai may be tried again because the law does not prohibit double jeopardy. In August 2005, the government dropped a second treason charge that had been based on claims that he urged violence to bring down the government in 2004.

Division in the Opposition

In late 2004, the MDC became increasingly divided in its strategy to defeat the Mugabe government. MDC officials initially decided that the party would not participate in the 2005 parliamentary campaign, unless the government took steps to assure a free and fair election. Several party members questioned this stance on grounds that non-participation would deprive the party of any influence in the next parliament. Some reportedly felt that a refusal to participate would hand control of parliament to Mugabe on a "silver platter." Tsvangirai supported a boycott, arguing that the elections should be postponed until substantial electoral reforms could be implemented. The party did eventually participate "under protest," but did not do as well as in previous polls.

In the months prior to the 2005 Senate elections, the MDC was once again divided on whether to participate. Supported by some civil society groups who suggested the elections were "meaningless" and "a waste of time and resources," Tsvangirai argued that participating in the Senate would legitimize previous "rigged" elections, and vowed instead to lead the opposition through mass action. He was opposed by a group of MDC politicians led by the party's secretary-general, Welshman Ncube, who had also been accused by the government of treason in 2003 (the charges were subsequently dropped), and Gibson Sibanda. In October, the party's national council voted 33-3 1 to participate in the election, but Tsvangirai overruled the vote and, reportedly in violation of the party's constitution, expelled 26 senior officials from the party. He announced the boycott, touring the country to encourage voters to stay home. The Ncube faction refused to accept their expulsion and fielded candidates in the Senate race, although they gained only seven seats.

Both factions held party conferences in early 2006; Tsvangirai was confirmed as the leader of one faction, while Ncube ceded control of the "pro-senate" faction to Arthur Mutambara, a noted student leader in the 1980s. The two factions attacked each other in the press, and there were allegations that the Tsvangirai faction was behind a violent July 2006 assault on Member of Parliament (MP) Trudy Stevenson and several other Mutambara supporters. Stevenson identified the youths who attacked her as known followers of the former labor leader, but Tsvangirai has denied the charges and denounced the beatings. Although Tsvangirai' s faction is reported to have the larger support base and the backing of the ZCTU, some observers suggest neither faction will be effective unless they can resolve their differences and reunite.

Opposition Defiance Against a Ban on Protests and Rallies

On February 22, 2007, the Zimbabwean government announced a three-month ban on political rallies and public demonstrations in Harare "due to the volatile situation in the country."[43] The MDC filed an appeal with the High Court to lift the ban, which coincided with an increase in public activity by the opposition and civic groups. On February 18, despite a High Court decision allowing Morgan Tsvangirai to launch his presidential campaign at a rally in Harare, police reportedly used batons and water cannons to break up the event. A rally planned by the Mutambara faction in Bulawayo was similarly dispersed, and numerous opposition supporters were arrested. The ban was announced three days later, and police subsequently arrested several hundred civic activists, according to press reports.

On March 11, 2007, police broke up a Save Zimbabwe Campaign prayer meeting attended by both Tsvangirai and Mutambara, arresting an estimated 50 members of the opposition and civil society, including both MDC leaders. Police shot and killed one opposition supporter after MDC youth reportedly began throwing stones at police. The following day, police arrested an estimated 240 opposition supporters during a demonstration protesting the March 11 crackdown. Media and human rights reports suggest that Tsvangirai was severely beaten while in custody, and he appeared in court on March 13 showing signs of head trauma.[44] Other opposition and civic leaders also reportedly sustained injuries after their arrest. The protestors were released into the custody of their lawyers on March 14 after prosecutors reportedly failed to appear at their court hearing. The Zimbabwean government contended that the MDC incited violence and was responsible for attacks on several civilian targets and a Harare police station.[45]

The March 11 incident spurred international media attention and drew considerable criticism from many world leaders. U.S. Secretary of State Condoleezza Rice issued a strong statement, saying, "The world community again has been shown that the regime of Robert Mugabe is ruthless and repressive and creates only suffering for the people of Zimbabwe."[46] U.N. Secretary-General Ban Ki-moon also condemned the "reported beating of those leaders in police custody" and criticized the ban, noting that "such actions violate the basic democratic right of citizens to engage in peaceful assembly."[47] Several of Zimbabwe's neighbors, including South Africa and Zambia, issued statements of concern regarding the incident, and Ghanaian President John Kufuor, then chairman of the African Union, called the event "very embarrassing."[48]

Political Violence

Human rights groups have documented numerous accounts of political violence in recent years. According to Freedom House, "Zimbabwe's descent into the ranks of the world's most repressive states continued unabated."[49] The State Department reported that Zimbabwe's government has "engaged in the pervasive and systematic abuse of human rights, which increased significantly during the year"and contends that "state-sanctioned use of excessive force increased, and security forces tortured members of the opposition, student leaders, and civil society activists," in 2007.[50] Amnesty International is similarly critical:

> The human rights situation continued to deteriorate, in a context of escalating poverty. Freedom of expression, assembly and association continued to be curtailed. Hundreds of people were arrested for participating or attempting to engage in peaceful protest. Police were accused of torturing human rights defenders in custody. The situation of thousands of people whose homes were destroyed as part of Operation Murambatsvina (Restore Order) in 2005 continued to worsen, with no effective solution planned by the authorities. The government continued to obstruct humanitarian efforts by the UN and by local and international non-governmental organizations.[51]

President Mugabe has repeatedly condoned police and military brutality against Zimbabwean citizens. In August 2006, during Heroes' Day, a holiday honoring war veterans, Mugabe warned that his security forces "will pull the trigger" against protesters.[52] A month later, in an incident caught on video, Zimbabwean police conducted a particularly violent crackdown against leaders of the Zimbabwe Congress of Trade Unions (ZCTU), who had planned a civic protest to highlight the impact of inflation on the country's citizenry. Mugabe sanctioned the police action, saying, "Some people are now crying foul that they were assaulted, yes you get a beating ... when the police say move, move, if you don't move, you invite the police to use force."[53] Subsequent mass ZCTU protests were not held.

Mugabe received international attention for his statement; the U.N. Country Team (UNCT) in Zimbabwe announced "a profound sense of dismay" over comments that "might be interpreted as condoning the use of force and torture to deal with peaceful demonstrations by its citizens."[54] The U.N. Special Rapporteur on Torture[55] has repeated a 2005 request for an invitation from Zimbabwe to investigate, and the Harare magistrate who heard the case against the ZCTU leaders has ordered an independent investigation into the allegations of police brutality.

The U.N. Rapporteur may have several other cases to investigate — the Zimbabwe Human Rights NGO Forum reports that there were 586 incidents of torture from January through December 2007, 855 incidents of assault, and 19 incidents of politically motivated abduction/kidnapping.[56] These figures suggest an marked increase in political violence from the 2006, during which there were 368 incidents of torture, 509 incidents of assault, and 11 incidents of politically motivated abduction/kidnapping.[57] Human rights activists suggest that abductions and beatings of opposition supporters appear to be "more systematic and widespread" since the events of March 2007.[58] Human Rights Watch reports that there has been an increase in incidents of violence in the 2008 pre-election period, despite provisions in the new Electoral Laws Amendment Act banning such acts and assurances by security officials that the government would take a "zero tolerance" approach to violence.[59]

Some reports suggest the government may be having difficulty paying its police and security forces, which rights activists infer could affect their willingness to suppress protests with violence or conduct other alleged rights violations. Nevertheless, reports suggest that police still play a significant role in political violence. The Geneva-based International Commission of Jurists, which investigated the May 2007 detention and beating of lawyers, expressed shock at the role police played in the attacks and at the "cavalier response of Zimbabwean authorities."[60]

HUMANITARIAN SITUATION

Operation Murambatsvina

In May 2005, the Government of Zimbabwe initiated Operation *Murambatsvina* (variously translated as "Restore Order" or "Clean Out the Filth"), a massive demolition program aimed at destroying allegedly illegal urban structures, such as informal housing and markets. By early July 2005, an estimated 700,000 urban Zimbabweans had been rendered homeless or unemployed by the operation, and an estimated 2.1 million (in total, almost 20% of the population) were indirectly affected by the demolitions.[61] These are considered "low-end estimates," and some reports suggest the numbers of those affected may be much higher.[62] According to some sources, 70% of the country's urban population may have lost shelter, while approximately 76% lost their source of income.[63] Police and military who carried out the event reportedly arrested forty thousand for allegedly illegal activities, and told those whose homes were destroyed to "return to their rural origins," although many had no rural home to which they could return.[64]

Operation Murambatsvina has had a severe impact on the nation's economy and on the livelihood of its citizens. For many, this was not the first time they had been forcibly removed from their homes. As a result of the 2000 land reform program, an estimated 400,000 black laborers on commercial farms lost their livelihoods and/or homes, and many fled to urban areas to find work. Political violence surrounding the 2002 elections also forced many from their homes, reportedly displacing more than 100,000.[65] In 2004, under a new phase of land resettlement, an estimated 500,000 who settled on farms during the 2000 invasions were evicted.[66] Many of these displaced inhabited the urban "slums" prior to the demolitions, making their living from trading on the black market. Given the collapse of the formal economy, 40% of the labor force was estimated to be informally employed prior to Murambatsvina, while 44% worked in the communal sector (including the agriculture industry), and 16% worked in the formal sector.[67] Of those living in towns and cities, an estimated 70% were involved in informal trading prior to the demolitions.

Political Motivations?

The government describes Murambatsvina as a program designed to restore the capital city to its former image as "the Sunshine City," ridding the country's urban areas of illegal structures that foster criminal activity and stemming the black market trade in foreign currency.[68] Launched shortly after the disputed 2005 parliamentary elections, many contend the demolitions were a political move aimed either at preventing mass protests over the growing economic crisis or at punishing the reputed urban support base of the MDC. The Harare Commission that initiated the campaign was established in order to contravene the authority of the elected City Council, of which the MDC held the majority. The mayor of Harare, an MDC politician who was elected by 80% of the vote, was fired in April 2004, along with 19 MDC-allied city councillors, after having been arrested in 2003 under POSA for holding a public meeting without prior state approval.

The legality of the Harare Commission, which was appointed by the Minister of Local Government, was challenged in a November 2003 high court ruling that found the Commission did not have the authority to fire the mayor. A new election was supposed to be held within 90 days, according to law, but when no election occurred, the Harare Commission was reappointed. The remaining MDC councillors resigned in protest. With the exception of Harare, the local authorities of the other areas (many of which are MDC-controlled) affected by Murambatsvina have reported that they were not informed of the demolitions prior to the event. The implications of this breakdown in governance are reflected by the United Nations, which found that Murambatsvina "was implemented in a highly polarized political climate characterized by mistrust, fear and a lack of dialogue between Government and local authorities, and between the former and civil society."[69]

The International Response

International reaction was highly critical. U.N. Secretary-General Kofi Annan named Tanzanian-born Anna Tibaijuka, Executive Director of UN-HABITAT, as the U.N. Special Envoy on Human Settlements Issues in Zimbabwe to investigate the humanitarian impact of the demolitions. Following a fact-finding mission to the country, she issued a comprehensive report, which concluded:

> Operation Restore Order, while purporting to target illegal dwellings and structures and to clamp down on alleged illicit activities, was carried out in an indiscriminate and unjustified manner, with indifference to human suffering and, in repeated cases, with disregard to several provisions of national and international legal frameworks.[70]

The report also described police preventing civil society and humanitarian organizations from assisting those affected by the demolitions, and suggested that the groups were operating in a "climate of fear" and practicing "'self-censorship' to avoid being closed down or evicted."[71] The Chairman of the African Union sent his own envoy, but he was prevented from conducting an assessment (see "International Perspectives," below). The presentation of the U.N. envoy's report to the U.N. Security Council stirred controversy as China, Algeria, Benin, and Russia objected to debate on the report. The majority of Security Council members voted to allow its discussion, albeit in a closed session. Secretary-General Annan also issued a strong statement condemning Murambatsvina, calling on the government of Zimbabwe to stop the evictions and allow unimpeded access for humanitarian assistance:

> "Operation Murambatsvina" has done a catastrophic injustice to as many as 700,000 of Zimbabwe's poorest citizens, through indiscriminate actions, carried out with disquieting indifference to human suffering. I call on the Government to stop these forced evictions and demolitions immediately, and to ensure that those who orchestrated this ill-advised policy are held fully accountable for their actions ... the Government must recognize the virtual state of emergency that now exists, allow unhindered access for humanitarian operations, and create conditions for sustainable relief and reconstruction.[72]

Continued Evictions and Operation Garikai

Many observers suggest the Zimbabwean government has done little to respond to the U.N. envoy's recommendations.[73] Reports suggest that forced evictions continued, despite government declarations to the contrary.[74] As was the case during the initial evictions, several thousand of those made homeless were taken, in some cases reportedly against their will, to police-run "transit camps" in late 2006. Conditions in these camps have been described as dire, often lacking shelter, water, or basic latrine facilities.[75] In keeping with the findings of the U.N. report, Amnesty International alleges that Zimbabwe has repeatedly prohibited aid organizations, including the United Nations, from providing the displaced with temporary shelters, such as tents, until permanent housing became available. Secretary-General Annan expressed his concern in October 2005 over the government's rejection of U.N. assistance to "tens of thousands," noting "there is no clear evidence that subsequent Government efforts have significantly benefitted these groups."[76] The United Nations was subsequently permitted to erect approximately 2,300 shelters, a fraction of their target of 40,000.[77]

In response to international criticism of Murambatsvina, the government announced a new housing scheme, Operation *Garikai*, in June 2005. Under *Garakai*, also known as "Hlalani Kuhle" (Live Well), new housing for those rendered homeless was to be built with public funds. The ambitious reconstruction program would allegedly create tens of thousands of new homes, but given the shortage of building materials and the government's budgetary problems, it is highly unlikely the original target of 5,275 homes will be met. Reports suggest that few houses have actually been completed, and, instead of going to victims of Murambatsvina, the newly built houses have been more often occupied by soldiers, police, and members of the ruling party.[78] The government denies these allegations.

Violations of Domestic and International Law

Human rights organizations have raised questions about how Zimbabwe and the international community should respond to what some have termed "crimes against humanity,"[79] as defined by Article 7 of the Rome Statute of the International Criminal Court (ICC),[80] and whether there is a "responsibility to protect"[81] those affected by Murambatsvina. Among the U.N. report recommendations, the envoy suggests:

> Although a case for crime against humanity under Article 7 of the Rome Statute might be difficult to sustain, the Government of Zimbabwe clearly caused large sections of its population serious suffering that must now be redressed with the assistance of the United Nations and the international community. The international community should encourage the Government to prosecute all those who orchestrated this catastrophe and those who may have caused criminal negligence leading to alleged deaths, if so confirmed by an independent internal inquiry/inquest. The international community should then continue to be engaged with human rights concerns in Zimbabwe in consensus building political forums such as the UN

Commission on Human Rights, or its successor, the African Union Peer Review Mechanism, and in the Southern African Development Community.

The report includes a legal analysis of Murambatsvina through international and regional, and national legal frameworks. Several domestic and international organizations, including the International Bar Association (IBA), have called for the Zimbabwean government to be brought before the ICC, not only for violations related to the demolitions, but also for the government's alleged support of political violence against its critics. Responding to President Mugabe' s comments supporting the beating of the ZCTU leaders in September 2006, the Executive Director of the IBA made the following statement:

> Mugabe' s statements add to the weight of evidence that torture and other serious violations of international law are sanctioned at the highest level in Zimbabwe. This underscores the urgent need for international and regional action to hold the Zimbabwean Government to account ... the torture of the trade union activists is not an isolated incident, but part of a dangerous and illegal system of repression which constitutes crimes against humanity in international law. Decisive action is required by both the United Nations and the African Union to end impunity and violence in Zimbabwe.[82]

Because Zimbabwe is not a signatory of the Rome Statute, a U.N. Security Council resolution would be needed for any referral to the ICC. Given the objections of some Security Council members to the envoy's report itself, which as stated above suggested an ICC case would be "difficult to sustain," it is unlikely such a referral would be made. The U.N. Envoy found that "The Government of Zimbabwe is collectively responsible for what has happened," but cautioned that "it appears there was no collective decision-making with respect to both the conception and implementation. Evidence suggests it was based on improper advice by a few architects of the operation."[83] According to one media source, though, Zimbabwe's State Security Minister has claimed, "All the decisions to do with the operation emanated from the politburo [the ruling party's inner cabinet] and were sent through me to the government."[84]

The government of Zimbabwe has yet to prosecute those who might be responsible for crimes related to Operation Murambatsvina or the subsequent evictions. The victims, in most cases, lack the financial resources to seek redress in the courts, although Zimbabwean human rights lawyers have represented groups of victims on several occasions. In one such case, in November 2005, residents of a Harare suburb were given a temporary stay of eviction by the High Court, but police ignored the court order and forcibly moved the group to a transit camp. The inability of the country's judicial system to protect its citizens or their property, or to provide due process to those seeking remedy or compensation, suggests a fundamental crisis in Zimbabwe's rule of law.

Zimbabwe's Food Crisis

Several Southern African countries have suffered from chronic food insecurity in recent years, stemming from a combination of weather-related and man-made factors, including prolonged drought, floods, poor economic performance, and the impact of HIV/AIDS.[85] Zimbabwe has been particularly hard hit. Grain silos across the country that once held strategic grain reserves three times the population's annual food needs now stand empty. Five million Zimbabweans, almost half the population, received food aid in early 2006. Experts attribute this food insecurity to unexpectedly severe crop failure,[86] but some suggest Murambatsvina and other government policies significantly limited the population's ability to feed itself, particularly in urban areas.[87] USAID and the World Food Program predict that over 4.1 million Zimbabweans, more than a third of the country's population, will need food assistance in early 2008.[88]

Although drought is partly to blame for the country's food shortages, analysts believe that disruptions to the farming sector resulting from Mugabe' s land seizure program are the main reason for reduced food production.[89] Nearly all of the country's 4,500 commercial farms have now been taken over; the government's land redistribution program is reportedly plagued by inefficiencies, with large portions of redistributed land not being actively farmed. Tractors and other inputs to production are reportedly in short supply. Thousands of experienced farm workers were reportedly forced to flee seized commercial farms, and many of those who now hold farmland have no agricultural expertise. The government's introduction of price controls in 2007 may further restrict production — the country's seed and fertilizer producers report that the controls have created "unrealistic prices," which in turn have caused shortages for the latest farming season.[90]

Operation Taguta

In late 2005, the Zimbabwean government established Operation *Taguta* (or "Eat Well"), a move seen by many as an acknowledgment that the government's farm resettlement policies had failed to meet the country's agricultural production needs. With food distribution already under the control of the Grain Marketing Board, led by military officers, the government established a command agriculture system, in which the military would be responsible for not only the distribution, but also the production of food. Since the program's inception, there have been numerous reports of the illegal seizure of farm equipment, the destruction of the fruit, vegetable, and other cash crops small-scale farmers grow to sell at market to support their families, and even army brutality against farmers. Some critics of the government suggest Operation Taguta was used by the government as an excuse to deploy military forces throughout the country to control the population.[91]

Food as a Political Weapon?

The Mugabe regime's stance on food aid leads many observers to suspect that food is being used as a political weapon, a charge the government denies.[92] Despite assessments by multiple international donor agencies suggesting the need for food assistance, President Mugabe confounded observers in recent years by repeatedly declaring the country was running a maize surplus and would not need food aid.[93] In 2004, the government stopped a U.N. food needs assessment and later halted general food aid distribution by donors (targeted food aid to vulnerable groups continued), despite independent estimates that suggested 4.8 million would require assistance.[94] In March 2005, the government finally acknowledged serious food shortages, but delayed in signing agreement to allow the World Food Program (WFP) and its implementing partners to provide assistance until December of that year.[95] Reports suggest the government continues to maintain tight control of food distributions.[96] The government has accused aid agencies of using food to turn Zimbabweans away from the ruling party.

Critics like Pius Ncube, former Catholic Archbishop of Bulawayo, have accused the government of distributing food only in areas where people would agree to vote for ZANU-PF. During past elections, civil rights groups and the opposition have reported instances of the ruling party holding campaign rallies in conjunction with government food distributions. In some areas, government officials distributing food required those in line to show a party card — and MDC supporters were reportedly turned away. Two 2005 court rulings supported these claims, finding that ZANU-PF candidates politicized food distribution and used violence against the opposition.[97]

HIV/AIDS

In the midst of its political and economic crisis, Zimbabwe is being ravaged by HIV/AIDS. One in five Zimbabweans is HIV positive. The United Nations Children's Fund (UNICEF) estimates that almost one quarter of

Zimbabwe's children are orphans (primarily attributable to AIDS), the highest percentage in the world.[98]

The epidemic is also causing a severe strain on the country's healthcare system; 75% of hospital admissions are AIDS-related, leaving few beds or resources for other patients. To compound this problem, the economic crisis has resulted in the exodus of many of the country's medical professionals. Of those who remain, many are infected with HIV themselves, leaving Zimbabwe to rely upon assistance from others. The AIDS epidemic is having a crippling effect on the economy- the inability of infected agricultural workers to adequately contribute to food production further hamstrings the struggling industry.

Although its infection rate remains high, Zimbabwe is the only country in Sub-Saharan Africa in which HIV prevalence and incidence rates have declined. While reports suggest evidence of changes in sexual behavior,[99] the country's high mortality rates also play a role in the decreased prevalence rate.[100] Zimbabwe's government has claimed significant resolve to fight the disease. The country was the first to introduce a tax to finance HIV/AIDS programs (3% on taxable income). President Mugabe announced in Zimbabwe's commitment to universal access to antiretroviral therapy (ART) by 2010. Despite this commitment, access to ART is low — an estimated one in seven HIV positive Zimbabweans is currently able to access the drugs.[101]

For those who are able to access treatment, the country's economic crisis is limiting its impact. Patients taking ART must maintain healthy diets for the treatment to be effective, but with malnutrition rates high, few are able to benefit. Murambatsvina reportedly displaced an estimated 80,000 infected with HIV/AIDS, leaving many not only food insecure but also without access to ART. Experts suggest this disruption in ART may lead to increased resistance in HIV-positive patients to the most common medication, Nevirapine.[102] The displacement and separation of families may also lead to an increase in unsafe sexual behavior, which could reverse the country's decreasing prevalence rate.

THE ECONOMY

The turmoil in Zimbabwe has led to a severe economic contraction, a sharp drop in living standards for the rural and urban poor, and a massive exodus of Zimbabweans in search of work. According to the Solidarity Peace Trust, founded by clergy from Zimbabwe and South Africa, over three million Zimbabweans are now living outside the country. The Trust calculates that this amounts to 25%-30% of the total population, or 60%-70% of productive adults.[103] Those forced to leave the country because of economic hardship often face difficult conditions because economic refugees are not entitled to political asylum. Many of those who remain behind now reportedly rely on remittances from family abroad.

The IMF and the World Bank

Dubbed "the world's fastest shrinking economy," Zimbabwe's Gross Domestic Product (GDP) has declined an estimated 40% since 1998.[104] World Bank and the International Monetary Fund (IMF) lending has been suspended since 2000 due to nonpayment of arrears, and foreign currency for essential imports, particularly fuel, is in extremely short supply. The IMF suggests that the inflation rate will not reverse without significant changes in government spending.[105] Zimbabweans continue to face steep rises in the prices of food and non-food items.

In December 2003, Mugabe selected Gideon Gono, credited with turning around a troubled commercial bank, as governor of the Reserve Bank of Zimbabwe. The move was welcomed by some, since Gono was regarded as a successful technocrat. However, critics maintain that his measures to fight corruption and discover illegally held foreign exchange are being used to damage government opponents and further the interests of ZANU-PF.[106] Regardless of Gono' s efforts, international assessments of Zimbabwe's economic prospects remain bleak. Ignoring the advice of the IMF, the government has refused to devalue the official exchange rate. Instead, in June 2006, Gono devalued the country's currency, the Zimbabwe dollar, removing three zeros in an effort to mitigate inflation.

Under "Operation Sunrise," the government printed new "rebased" currency, known as "little heroes," in an effort to combat corruption and money laundering, according to the government.[107] Zimbabweans were given only 21 days to exchange their old currency. Individuals were restricted from exchanging more than Z$100 million (USD$ 1000) of the old notes without clearance from tax authorities (companies were allowed to exchange Z$5 billion). Police arrested more than 3,000 at roadblocks for holding currency over the individual limit and seized a reported $40 million.[108] Analysts suggest the devaluation has done little to reverse the foreign exchange rate shortages.[109]

Zimbabwe is currently restricted from borrowing from the IMF, to which the country still owes an estimated $119 million. The government paid $120 million in 2005 and $9 million in 2006 to settle other outstanding arrears with the Fund and to avoid compulsory withdrawal from the IMF. The source of the funds used to pay the IMF debt has been a source of considerable speculation in the media.[110] Mugabe has dubbed the IMF a "political instrument" and "monster" for regime change.[111]

Zimbabwe also owes an estimated $409 million to the World Bank and $300 million to the African Development Bank.

Attempts to Revive Agriculture Industry

In addition to the government's attempts to revive its flagging agriculture industry through the introduction of a command agriculture system (see "Food Crisis" section, above), the administration has introduced long-term leases to provide security of tenure for farmers willing to cultivate land nationalized in the 2005 constitutional amendment. One of the unintended side effects of Mugabe's 2000 land reform strategy, which resulted in the abolition of land tenure, was that farmers were unable to use their land as collateral to obtain bank loans to invest in their farms. As a result, few commercial farmers were able to find the capital to maintain productivity. The government began to distribute 99-year leases in November 2006, and among the initial recipients were 19 white farmers, which came as a shock to many after Mugabe declared in July 2005 that his land reform program would be complete only when there was "not a single white on the farms."[112] There are currently less than 600 white farmers left in Zimbabwe. Some suggest financial institutions may be reluctant to accept the new leases as collateral, given that the government reserves the right to cancel the lease if it deems the farm unproductive.

The government also announced in May 2007 its intention to ration electricity to households across the country in order to divert its dwindling supplies for irrigation of Zimbabwe's winter wheat crop.[113] More recent electricity shortages, caused by supply cuts from Mozambique, South Africa, and Zambia, have compounded Zimbabwe's economic woes, cutting the production capacity of the manufacturing and mining sectors by as much 50%, according to some reports.[114]

The Mining Industry and Nationalization of Foreign Companies

While the country's agriculture industry founders, its mining industry has continued to bring much-needed income into Zimbabwe. Mining accounts for almost half of Zimbabwe's total foreign currency revenues. In early 2006, the government announced plans to take a 51% share of all foreign-owned mines for local black investors; 25% of that share would be acquired at no cost to the government, and mines that refused to part with their shares would be expropriated. After industry officials cautioned that the plan would deter foreign investment, the proposal was modified, allowing firms that invested in community projects to keep their majority share. Parliament is expected to consider the legislation in 2008. They voted to approve similar plans to take a majority share in all foreign-owned businesses in September 2007; the legislation became law in March 2008. The Zimbabwe government insists that it will not expropriate foreign-owned companies and that the law will not be applied to every company, but rather "on the basis of capital (investment) and employment levels."[115] Critics argue the law will further deter much-needed foreign investment.

The government has taken steps to crackdown on illegal mining. Police arrested an estimated 20,000 illegal miners, in late 2006, including several hundred reportedly legal small-scale miners, confiscating gold, diamonds, emeralds, and gold ore. Since the collapse of the formal economy, many of the country's unemployed have resorted to illegal mining, selling their goods on the black market. According to reports, most of the miners were released after paying fines.

The Kimberly Process, an international government certification scheme designed to prevent trade in conflict diamonds, is investigating allegations that "blood diamonds" from the Democratic Republic of Congo (DRC) are being smuggled along with rough stones from Zimbabwe into South Africa for export. If the allegations are proven, Zimbabwe's legal diamond exports could be banned. The government has dismissed the claims as a western attempt to promote regime change. Zimbabwe has been previously linked to conflict diamonds; senior officials were named in a 2003 U.N. report for profiting from illicit diamond trade during Zimbabwe's military operations in the DRC.[116]

"Look East" Policy

Blaming the United States, the United Kingdom, and other western governments for the country's economic crisis, Mugabe has sought to engender investment and trade opportunities with Asia, particularly China. Dubbed the "Look East" policy, Mugabe' s efforts have been criticized by his own party as insufficient to address the economy's slide. In December 2006, the Parliamentary Portfolio Committee on Budget, Finance, and Economic Development, chaired by a ZANU-PF MP, accused the central bank governor of exacerbating inflation with "quasi-fiscal activities" and warned the administration that "the Far East destinations be viewed as a market in its infancy and that the traditional market of the West should not be neglected as the nation moves toward regularizing relations with the international community."[117]

The Military and the Economy

Critics contend that President Mugabe is buying the continued loyalty of the country's security forces through patronage and bribery.[118] Some observers suggest that loyalty of the security forces may come at a heavy cost to the economy. In 2006 the government reportedly spent more than $20 million to purchase new cars for police, military and intelligence officers. The security forces and civil service also reportedly received an almost 300% pay raise to counter record desertion rates. Observers continue to speculate on how the government will pay for its military purchases from China, including $240 million in fighter jets.

In addition to allegations of land and housing handouts to security personnel, critics of the government highlight a significant number of current and former military officers who have been appointed to civilian government positions. Current or former military officers currently control the Ministries of Energy and Industry, the Zimbabwe Revenue Authority (in charge of tax collection), the electoral commission, the state railway, the Grain Marketing Board, and the parks authority, and several are serving in the Senate and ambassadorial posts abroad.

As the economy continues to collapse, there are signs that the government may be running out of funds to maintain its security forces. During a parliamentary hearing in May 2007, the Defense Secretary reportedly suggested that soldiers were dissatisfied with their low salaries and that the forces were running out of food and might have to suspend training if new funds were not released.[119] Later that month, Zimbabwean intelligence officials reportedly uncovered a coup plot led by several senior military officials. Unconfirmed reports suggest that as many as 400 members of the army, air force, and police may have been involved in the plan, which allegedly aimed to remove Mugabe and to install Emmerson Mnangagwa as president. Mnangagwa, who has reportedly long sought to succeed Mugabe, denied any knowledge of the plot. Other sources suggest Vice President Joice Mujuru and her husband were behind the coup attempt and used Mnangagwa's name to discredit him. At least five men, including a retired army captain, were arrested and charged with treason.[120] The accused have denied the charges. Neither Mnangagwa nor the Mujurus were officially accused of involvement, although some reports suggest Solomon Mujuru may have been placed under house arrest for a limited time.[121]

International Perspectives

The international community appears divided on how to respond to Zimbabwe's persistent political and economic crisis. In general, Western nations and institutions have expressed opposition to Mugabe's methods of rule, and have pursued policies intended to pressure the Zimbabwe government for reforms. In contrast, the Mugabe government has enjoyed considerable sympathy in Africa, where he is viewed as an elder statesman and a leader of the anti-colonial struggle, and among the Non-Aligned nations generally. This is changing to an extent, however, with some African leaders concluding that the Zimbabwe situation is damaging to Africa's interests and that political and economic reforms are needed. Nevertheless, African countries supported Zimbabwe in its successful bid to chair the United Nations Commission on Sustainable Development in May 2007, allegedly to show African solidarity against American and European opposition.

U.S. Policy

The United States has been critical of the Mugabe regime for its poor human rights record and lack of respect for the rule of law. Key elements of U.S. policy toward Zimbabwe include the imposition of targeted sanctions against high-ranking ZANU-PF members and their affiliates, support for South Africa to spearhead an African effort to restore democracy, and the provision of assistance intended to help the country's poor and strengthen civil society. Secretary of State Condoleezza Rice told the Senate Foreign Relations Committee during her 2005 confirmation hearing, that Zimbabwe was one of six "outposts of tyranny" worldwide and that the United States stood with the oppressed people there.[122] These remarks provoked an angry personal response from Mugabe.[123] Thomas Woods, then-Deputy Assistant Secretary of State for African Affairs, was similarly critical, suggesting that Zimbabwe "has now become a textbook case of bad and illegitimate government."[124]

Sanctions

The Mugabe administration has routinely blamed its economic crisis on sanctions from the west. The United States does not currently have trade sanctions against Zimbabwe, with the exception of a ban on transfers of defense items and services to the country. The U.S. government has, however, cancelled all non-humanitarian government-to-government aid. In 2006, Zimbabwe was found to be in violation of crimes related to human trafficking and was subject to sanction under the Trafficking Victims Protection Act of 2000 (P.L. 106-386) for FY2007.[125] In 2007, the State Department found that Zimbabwe was "making significant efforts" to combat trafficking, and Zimbabwe was moved from a "Tier 3" to a "Tier 2" designation.[126] Zimbabwe is not eligible for trade benefits under the African Growth and Opportunity Act (AGOA) because and its poor record of economic management and human rights abuses.

President Bush announced a renewal of U.S. sanctions against ZANU-PF leaders in March 2007. The sanctions are intended to punish those responsible for Zimbabwe's difficulties without harming the Zimbabwe population at large. The initial sanctions, imposed in 2003, ban travel to the United States by "senior members of the government of Robert Mugabe and others ... who formulate, implement, or benefit from policies that undermine or injure Zimbabwe's democratic institutions or impede the transition to a multi-party democracy." Persons who benefit financially from business dealings with such individuals are also banned, as are the spouses of people in either group. In 2003, the President issued an executive order freezing assets held in the United States by 75 high-ranking Zimbabwe officials and Mugabe's wife, Grace.[127] Nine firms and farms were added in 2004, and the list was further expanded in November 2005 to block the assets of 128 individuals and 33 entities. The President's executive order also allows the Secretary of the Treasury, in consultation with the Secretary of State, to go beyond previous authority and block the property of additional persons who "have engaged in actions or policies to undermine Zimbabwe's democratic processes or institutions," their immediate family members, and any persons assisting them.[128] President Bush added an additional 38 names to the travel ban list in December 2007.

Congressional Response

Congress made clear its opposition to Mugabe' s policies in the Zimbabwe Democracy and Economic Recovery Act of 2001 (P.L. 107-99), which criticized "economic mismanagement" and "undemocratic practices" in Zimbabwe. This legislation called for consultations with allies on economic sanctions and a travel ban. In the 109th Congress, the U.S. House of Representatives passed H.Res. 409 in December 2005, condemning Operation Murambatsvina, which the resolution termed a "humanitarian disaster that has compounded the country's humanitarian food and economic crises." The resolution also called on the U.N. and African regional bodies to investigate the impact of the demolitions and requested that the Administration use its influence to advocate further action by the IMF against the Zimbabwean government. Senator Russ Feingold (D-WI) introduced S.Amdt. 1254, which was included in the final version of the FY2006 foreign operations appropriations bill (P.L. 109-102). This amendment provided $4 million for democracy and governance activities in Zimbabwe. The Senate Subcommittee on African Affairs held a hearing on Zimbabwe's political and economic crisis in June 2001. The House Subcommittee on Africa has likewise held hearings on challenges to democracy in Zimbabwe: in June 2000 prior to the parliamentary elections, in February 2002 prior to Zimbabwe's presidential elections, and in April 2005 following the parliamentary elections.

On April 17, 2007, the House of Representatives passed H.Con.Res. 100, sponsored by Representative Tom Lantos, condemning the Zimbabwean government's recent actions against opposition and civil society activists. In June 2007, the Senate passed parallel legislation, S.Con.Res. 25, introduced by Senator Barack Obama. Senator Hillary Rodham Clinton has introduced S. 1500, the Support for Democracy and Human Rights in Zimbabwe Act of 2007, which would authorize up to $10 million to support democracy and human rights programs in the country.

U.S. Support for African Diplomacy

During President Bush's visit to South Africa in 2003, he praised the work of President Thabo Mbeki as the "point man" in seeking a Zimbabwe solution. The statement suggested to some that the United States was stepping back from a lead role on the Zimbabwe issue and would accede to Mbeki' s "quiet diplomacy" (see "South Africa" section, below) as the best means of achieving reform in Zimbabwe.[129] Mbeki reportedly assured President Bush at that time that he would be able to bring about talks between ZANU-PF and the MDC, which did not occur until 2007. In 2004, the current U.S. Assistant Secretary of State for Africa and then Ambassador to South Africa, Jendayi Frazer, called for the formation of a "coalition of the willing" to deal with Zimbabwe. Ambassador Frazer reiterated South Africa's position of leverage, and insisted more needed to be done by African states to return Zimbabwe to democracy.[130]

U.S. Assistance

The United States remains the leader in humanitarian relief aid to the Zimbabwean people, supplying more than $400 million in food aid and disaster assistance since 2002. In addition to food aid, the United States provided $23.2 million in bilateral assistance for Zimbabwe in FY2007 and an estimated $22.9 million in FY2008. The Administration has requested $45.4 million for FY2009. The State Department stated in its FY2008 Congressional Budget Justification (CBJ) that supplemental assistance will be requested if elections are held during the fiscal year that result in the election of a "reform-minded" government.[131] Similar language was used in the FY2009 request, which states,

> If elections do not occur in 2008, or if elections continue the status quo, FY 2009 programming... will be reassessed to determine the most promising course to assist the democratic opposition to survive and to deepen

> its voice, thereby maintaining pressure on the GOZ to reform. Additionally, under a no-change scenario, the United States will promote a continuing dialogue with domestic and regional audiences on economic mismanagement, political manipulation, and human rights abuses.

Zimbabwe is not among the countries eligible to participate in the Millennium Challenge Account program, nor is it a focus country for the President's Emergency Plan for AIDS Relief.

USAID continues to support local democracy advocates in Zimbabwe through a variety of programs aimed at ensuring media freedom and strengthening civil society and the legislative process. USAID partners were reportedly instrumental in documenting the demolitions and human rights violations during Operation Murambatsvina and assisting in relief efforts. Legal restrictions continue to limit the ability of journalists and independent newspapers to provide alternative source for news, and the Zimbabwean government controls all domestic radio and television broadcasting stations. USAID provides funding for Voice of America to broadcast Studio 7, a daily program on shortwave and AM radio that USAID describes as "the principal source of independent electronic media in the country." Studio 7, along with UK-based Shortwave (SW) Radio Africa and the Dutch-funded Voice of the People (VOP) have had their broadcasts periodically interrupted by the Mugabe government using Chinese jamming equipment.

The U.S. State Department warns that travelers suspected of having a "bias" against the government may be refused entry to Zimbabwe.[132] In 2006, a delegation of the U.S. Coalition of Black Trade Unionists (CBTU), led by AFL-CIO Vice President William Lucy, was expelled from the country. Then-U.S. Ambassador Christopher Dell said,

> Clearly, the Zimbabwe government's decision not to honor the delegation's visas is the result of the events of 13 September, when security forces brutally suppressed planned peaceful demonstrations by the Zimbabwe Congress of Trade Unions.... This transparent attempt to deflect international attention from the vicious beatings is itself an example of the Zimbabwean government's repression and of its fear of the truth.... There is increasing acknowledgment that a man who was regarded as a liberator of his people is an oppressor.[133]

Other International Perspectives

United Kingdom

In 2002, in conjunction with the United States and the European Union, the British Parliament imposed targeted sanctions on leading members and affiliates of the ZANU-PF regime, as well an arms embargo and an asset freeze. The UK has imposed travel bans on over 100 members of the ZANUPF and close affiliates of the party. Britain continues to provide humanitarian aid in Zimbabwe. Concurrently, the UK maintains its willingness to release funds to Zimbabwe to pay for parts of an orderly land redistribution program if Mugabe retires and the rule of law is returned. Mugabe was extremely hostile toward former British Prime Minister Tony Blair, a persistent critic. Speaking at his 81st birthday celebration, Mugabe said the upcoming election would "kill once and for all the machinations of that man in Number 10 Downing Street, who for some reason thinks he has the divine power to rule Zimbabwe and Britain.... On March 31, we must dig a grave not just six feet but 12 feet and bury Mr. Blair and the Union Jack."[134] Current Prime Minister Gordon Brown has maintained his predecessor's position, boycotting the December 2007 EU-Africa Summit to protest Mugabe's attendance.

European Union

The European Union was among the first to take action against Mugabe's regime. The EU imposed targeted sanctions on 19 members of Zimbabwe's elite and their spouses after pulling the EU election observer team out of Zimbabwe in February 2002. These "light" sanctions were upgraded by the EU to target 35 Zimbabwean leaders, and have been renewed yearly, most recently in February 2007. Current EU sanctions include a travel ban on 130 members and beneficiaries of the ZANU-PF, an arms embargo, and an asset freeze. Mugabe defied the travel ban in 2005 to attend the funeral of Pope John Paul II. The EU continues to put pressure on the ZANU-PF government to hold talks with the MDC, while at the same time providing humanitarian assistance to benefit Zimbabwe's poor.

France is generally seen as favoring more engagement with the Mugabe regime than Britain or other EU members, and it lifted travel restrictions against Mugabe for a visit in 2005. France justified the move by arguing that the inclusion of Mugabe rather than isolation would provide a quicker path to easing the crisis. Cynics suggest that France may see engagement with Zimbabwe as a means of extending French influence in southern Africa, where it has historically not had a major role. Nevertheless, France has publicly stressed the need for dialogue with the opposition before Zimbabwe can improve relations with the international community, and it declined to invite Zimbabwe to the Franco-Africa Summit in February 2007.[135]

Commonwealth

The Commonwealth of Nations sent a team of observers to the March 2002 presidential election in Zimbabwe, and the group found "that the conditions in Zimbabwe did not adequately allow for the free expression of the will of the electors."[136] Consequently, a special committee appointed to monitor and respond to the vote, consisting of Australia, South Africa and Nigeria, determined that Zimbabwe would be suspended from the Commonwealth for one year. The suspension was the first public action against Mugabe by a body that included influential African countries. In December 2003, the Commonwealth, including 19 other African members, voted to suspend Zimbabwe indefinitely. On this occasion, the decision was strongly criticized by South Africa's President Mbeki, who had by then committed to his policy of quiet diplomacy, and by other governments in southern Africa. Mugabe responded by withdrawing Zimbabwe from the Commonwealth and ruling out any further discussions or a possible return.[137] Some speculated, as a result, that the Commonwealth's action had backfired by placing Zimbabwe fully outside the bounds of its influence. Others argued that indefinite suspension by a body including many African members had important symbolic value in Africa and worldwide.

China and Iran

While many western governments have moved to isolate the Mugabe regime, China and Iran have strengthened ties and deepened their involvement in Zimbabwe's economy. China, which became active on the continent in the 1950s and 1960s to gain global influence, now looks to Africa for natural resources to meet the needs of its growing population. A longtime ally of ZANU-PF, which it backed during the liberation struggle, China is reported to be Zimbabwe's second largest trading partner and its largest investor.[138] Many observers see Zimbabwe's platinum concessions as a major draw for Beijing, and Chinese firms are playing roles in the cell phone industry, as well as in television, radio, and power generation. China holds controlling interest in the country's only electricity generator.

Some critics worry China's investment in Zimbabwe comes without the "strings attached" that Western governments might require, such as commitments to human rights, accountability, and anti-corruption. Arms agreements between China and Zimbabwe have attracted considerable attention in recent years, as most Western governments continue to enforce an arms embargo against the country. Zimbabwe's $240 million purchase of twelve Chinese fighter jets has drawn questions from analysts as to why a country that faces no immediate external threat from its neighbors would need such an air force.[139] Reports indicate that Zimbabwe has also ordered riot gear, water cannons, armored vehicles, and AK-47 rifles from China. How impoverished Zimbabwe could pay for arms from China is a subject of much speculation; Defense Ministry officials have admitted to being in arrears for the 2005 arms purchases. Some observers suspect that the acquisitions are covered in some way by China's growing economic role in Zimbabwe.[140]

In the face of Western condemnation and isolation, Zimbabwe has also found an ally in Iran. During a 2006 visit to Tehran, President Mugabe reportedly secured commitments from Iran for direct aid and Iranian assistance to its energy, agriculture, and mining industries. Reports indicate that Iran may also provide technical assistance to Zimbabwe to revive the country's only oil refinery, built 40 years ago to process Iranian crude. Most of Zimbabwe's fuel comes by road from South Africa, but the country has insufficient foreign currency to import fuel in bulk through a pipeline from the nearest port, Beira, Mozambique to Zimbabwe.

In spite of Mugabe' s assurances of Iranian assistance, some observers suggest Iran may not meet his expectations. Despite an agreement signed by the two countries in 2005, little financial assistance appears to have been provided. As one economic advisor points out, "At the end of the day, whether its China or Iran, investors want one thing: a return on their investment and they do not seem to believe they can get that return (from Zimbabwe)."[141] Likewise, Mugabe, traveling to Beijing in 2005 to request assistance to deal with the country's foreign exchange shortfall and fuel shortage, received a scant $6 million for grain imports reportedly because Zimbabwe was deemed unworthy of significant investment.[142] Although Mugabe did secure a $200 million buyer credit loan from China to promote agricultural production (reportedly the largest loan to Zimbabwe since western donors ceased lending in 1999), China has dismissed reports that the countries were negotiating a much larger $2 billion loan meant to revive the country's flagging economy.[143]

In addition to investment and economic assistance, Zimbabwe's Asian partners have offered diplomatic support. A Chinese official visiting in 2004 said that his government "appreciates the reasons for the land issue" and was opposed to any interference by foreign governments.[144] China played a lead role in trying to quiet U.N. efforts to condemn Zimbabwe for Murambatsvina, and is expected to veto any proposed action by the Security Council to punish the Mugabe Administration. Iranian President Mahmoud Ahmadinejad expressed support during Mugabe's visit, saying "We believe Zimbabweans have every right to defend their sovereignty and land. We are happy that Zimbabwe has once again taken control over its resources and we support the land redistribution programme ... We strongly condemn the bullying tactics of a number of (Western) governments against Zimbabwe."[145]

Nigeria

Although an observer team from Nigeria endorsed the 2002 presidential election in Zimbabwe, Nigeria's former president, Olusegun Obasanjo, attempted to mediate the country's crisis. He was reportedly concerned about the consequences of the Zimbabwe situation for the credibility of the New Partnership for Africa's Development (NEPAD). NEPAD is an initiative aimed at demonstrating Africa's capabilities for resolving its own problems in exchange for increased aid, trade, and investment.[146] Obasanjo supported Zimbabwe's suspension from the Commonwealth, and in 2004, he held a long discussion with Tsvangirai and an MDC delegation in the Nigerian capital. The Nigerian leader then took the Zimbabwe visitors on a personal tour of his farm — an unusual privilege.[147] After the 2005 elections, Obasanjo met again with Tsvangirai, and the government-owned Herald newspaper accused the Nigerian president of funding the MDC.[148] The country's new president, Umaru Yar'Adua, has expressed his own concern with the situation in Zimbabwe, telling journalists at a German-African summit in October 2007 that developments in the country were "not in conformity with the rule of law."[149]

South Africa

President Thabo Mbeki' s "quiet diplomacy" toward Zimbabwe has drawn criticism from some for its slow pace and seeming lack of results. However, some analysts point out that Mbeki's reluctance to openly confront or condemn President Mugabe is understandable on a number of grounds. Mugabe lent aid and shelter to the African National Congress (ANC), now the ruling party in South Africa, during its long struggle against white minority rule, creating a bond of gratitude. Mugabe enjoys considerable popularity around Africa and in South Africa itself, not least because of his moves to seize lands owned by comparatively wealthy white farmers, and this may constrain Mbeki as well.

Nonetheless, many are dissatisfied that South Africa, which is immensely more powerful than neighboring Zimbabwe, and which has extensive control over Zimbabwe's transport links to the outside world, as well as over its electricity supplies, has not been able to do more to improve the Zimbabwe situation. As Zimbabwe's largest trading partner, many consider South Africa in a position to exert substantial leverage. At the same time, South Africa must weigh the unintended effects of such leverage — state collapse across its northern border could produce a sharp increase in illegal migration and have a substantial impact on South Africa. Some estimate that three million Zimbabweans have fled into the country, which is reportedly deporting an average of 3.900 Zimbabweans per week.[150]

Through his policy of engagement, President Mbeki has attempted to bring the Zimbabwean government and the MDC together to discuss Zimbabwe's future.

Mbeki' s offer of economic incentives and an exit strategy for Mugabe in exchange for negotiations with the opposition and a commitment to free and fair elections have, to date, been unsuccessful. In 2005, as the IMF threatened to expel Zimbabwe from the Fund for debt payment arrears, the country requested a loan from South Africa for fuel, food, and electricity, as well as to address the IMF payments. Amid rumors that the South African government would make any loan conditional on economic and political reforms, the negotiations stalled and Mugabe found another source from which to repay the IMF dues.[151] In early 2006 speech, Mugabe warned Mbeki that he should "keep away" from interference in Zimbabwe's affairs.

Mbeki' s Zimbabwe policies have drawn criticism from within his country; former President Nelson Mandela, Nobel laureate Archbishop Desmond Tutu, former opposition leader Tony Leon, and even the ANC's ally, the Congress of South African Trade Unions (COSATU), have been vocal detractors. COSATU, South Africa's powerful labor confederation, strongly opposes the quiet diplomacy policy. A certain sympathy on the part of COSATU toward the MDC may be inevitable, since the MDC has its roots in the union movement. COSATU delegations have been forcibly expelled from Zimbabwe twice, first in 2004 and more recently in late 2006, when COSATU members traveled to Harare to express their support for the ZCTU after the incidents of police violence. One COSATU leader remarked, "we are not quiet diplomats," and "we will not keep mum when freedom does not lead to respect for workers and human rights."[152] When the Mbeki government issued a terse initial statement following the March 2007 arrest of MDC and civil society activists, COSATU criticized the government for a "disgraceful" response, "in the face of such massive attacks on democracy and human rights, especially coming from those who owed so much to international solidarity when South Africans were fighting for democracy and human rights against the apartheid regime."[153]

Defenders of President Mbeki' s approach argue that he is the only leader with the influence and prestige needed to sway Mugabe. Some claim that Mbeki and South African diplomats have already made a contribution in Zimbabwe — helping to prevent the country from slipping into anarchy in 2002, for example.[154] Some observers expressed hope for Mbeki' s mediation role when the President and Morgan Tsvangirai met in October 2004, after Tsvangirai's acquittal. Tsvangirai, who had been critical of quiet diplomacy in the past, said after the meeting that he welcomed President Mbeki's efforts to mediate.[155] But Mbeki stunned the MDC and many supporters of democracy in Zimbabwe in March 2005, when he told a press conference that he had "no reason to think that anyone in Zimbabwe will militate in a way so that the elections will not be free and fair." He insisted that "there will be a free and fair election in Zimbabwe" and that "things like access to the public media, things like violence-free election have been addressed."[156] Earlier, he had termed Secretary Rice's description of Zimbabwe as an outpost of tyranny as "an exaggeration."[157] These remarks have left critics questioning the substance behind Mbeki' s diplomacy.

The future of South Africa's policy toward Zimbabwe may be determined by Mbeki's successor. Among the possible candidates, former Deputy President Jacob Zuma, who has been plagued by scandal, was elected as president of the ANC in December 2007.[158] Zuma has referred to the Zimbabwean president as "a monster," but has defended Mbeki's quiet diplomacy[159]. Other ANC leaders, including businessman Tokyo Sexwale, who spent ten years as a political prisoner with Nelson Mandela, have criticized Mbeki's policy, saying, "When a freedom fighter takes a wrong step, it is time for other freedom fighters to stand up and say 'we know you are a great man, but we cannot support what you are doing.'"[160] He has suggested that the Zimbabwean government may be ignoring Mbeki's efforts, and that it may be time to "turn up the volume."[161]

The African Union

The African Union (AU) and its predecessor, the Organization of African Unity (OAU), have been supportive of Mugabe in the past. In 2002, an OAU observer team labeled Mugabe's election victory legitimate, free, and fair. In July 2004, when the AU allowed a report critical of the Mugabe regime to be circulated at its annual summit, some believed the regional body might be indicating a change in its approach. The 114-page report, prepared by a delegation from the African Commission for Human and People's Rights (ACHPR) that visited Zimbabwe in 2002, reportedly criticized the Zimbabwe government for police abuses, press censorship, and compromising the judiciary.[162] The AU tabled the report at the summit, however, and declared it would keep its contents secret until Zimbabwe has had a chance to respond in detail. According to some media reports, the Zimbabwean government used procedural regulations and technicalities to prevent its release.[163] The ACHPR passed a resolution in December 2005 calling on the "government of Zimbabwe to respect the fundamental rights and freedoms of expression" and to allow a second fact-finding mission to enter the country. The ACHPR resolution was hailed by human rights advocates, who suggested, "This will exert a lot of pressure on Zimbabwe - this is the first time such a significant body, so close to African heads of state, observes and condemns such defiance of human rights compliance."[164] But like the previous report, the second mission's findings were rejected by the AU's Council of Ministers in 2006 because of "irregularities and procedural flaws."[165]

Some observers and international human rights organizations such as the International Press Institute (IPI), suggest that the AU's repeated rejection of ACHPR resolutions on Zimbabwe tarnishes the integrity of the body. As one AU official warned, "If we continue to throw out every human rights report that comes before us, people out there will stop taking us seriously."[166] IPI also suggests that refusal of the AU to act on the ACHPR resolutions or to condemn human rights abuses in Zimbabwe damages the credibility of the African Peer Review Mechanism (APRM) initiative, a vital part of the New Partnership for Africa's Development (NEPAD).[167]

Criticism from the AU may have little effect on Mugabe regardless, unless it is accompanied by more substantial policy changes toward his administration. Zimbabwe has routinely ignored its detractors and frequently denies those who might be critical of the regime access to the country. In 2005, AU Commission Chairman Alpha Konare sent Tom Nyanduga, Special Rapporteur on Refugees, Internally Displaced Persons, and Asylum Seekers in Africa, as his envoy to investigate Operation Murambatsvina. The Zimbabwean government prevented Nyanduga from conducting his assessment and deported him, accusing the envoy of "western collusion and agenda adoption."[168]

SADC

Many of the 14 members of the Southern African Development Community (SADC) are linked to Zimbabwe by a common historical experience, as well as cultural and economic ties, and the organization has been seen as disinclined to condemn the actions of President Mugabe' s regime. At its August 2004 summit in Mauritius, SADC approved new electoral principles and guidelines for all its member nations.[169] Analysts were hopeful that these rules might motivate meaningful democratic reforms in Zimbabwe, particularly since they laid out detailed guidelines for SADC observer missions.[170] The signatory countries, including Zimbabwe, are pledged to allow SADC observers freedom of movement and access. As noted above, the SADC observer delegation's favorable report for Zimbabwe's 2005 elections was considered by critics of the Mugabe administration to be disappointing.

Although Mugabe' s neighboring leaders have not singled him out for criticism, they do appear increasingly concerned with the impact of Zimbabwe's crisis on their own countries. Southern African leaders blamed Zimbabwe and Swaziland for undermining economic growth in the region at a SADC Summit in Lesotho in 2006.

Botswana has spoken out in the past on regional problems attributed to Mugabe' s policies, including the burden placed on the country by Zimbabwe's refugees. In March 2007, following the arrest of Tsvangirai and other opposition members,

Tanzanian President Jakaya Kikwete traveled to Harare to discuss the incident, and after the SADC summit, President Mbeki was nominated as mediator.

PROSPECTS FOR THE FUTURE

The future of Zimbabwe, in the short term, appears grave. Inflation and the cost of living remain on the rise, and the country's agriculture industry shows little sign of recovery. Prospects for Zimbabwe's youngest generation are equally grim. Primary school attendance has reportedly dropped almost 25% since 2000 (some reports suggest enrollment may have dropped a further 25% as a result of Murambatsvina), and the cost of school fees has risen exponentially. Many families are unable to afford basic food items, not to mention medicines or doctors. Analysts have cited a number of reasons for Zimbabwe's economic problems, including recurrent drought, difficulties encountered in implementing economic reforms, and industrial competition from comparatively cheap South African imports.[171] At the same time, analysts place considerable responsibility for Zimbabwe's problems on the policies adopted and actions taken by the government since 1997. The government has taken some fiscal measures to reverse the economic downturn, but as hyperinflation continues to rise, they have been largely ineffective.

The government of Zimbabwe has displayed little respect for the rule of law, which has, according to reports, in turn deterred desperately needed foreign investors. While President Mugabe' s allies may maintain their diplomatic solidarity, financial support could dwindle if they do not see a return on their investments. Likewise, the African solidarity on which Mugabe has relied may be waning as countries consider the impact of his policies on their own countries. Nigeria, Botswana, and Zambia, for example, have become increasingly critical. Experts will watch with interest as South Africa's President Thabo Mbeki prepares to retire, which could precipitate a change in the country's policy toward its neighbor.

Ultimately, Mugabe' s greatest challenge may come from within. If reports of frustration within his own party are accurate, the President may find it more difficult to mobilize party resources for this campaign than in past elections. If the GDP continues its decline, his government will also find itself with dwindling resources from which to draw to maintain support from its civil servants and its security forces.

There have already been signs of unrest — doctors in public hospitals across the country went on strike for better wages in 2007, as did workers at Zimbabwe's only electricity provider, leading to power outages throughout the country. The country's teachers went on strike in early 2008. Over 1,000 soldiers have reportedly deserted, fleeing to South Africa.[172] Nevertheless, the opposition remains divided and, some observers contend, disorganized. The Mutambara faction proved unable to defeat ZANU-PF electorally in late 2005, and neither faction has been able to win seats in recent by-elections.

As Zimbabwe's economy continues to collapse, the country's political situation may be approaching a critical juncture. Some analysts suggest that if the March 2008 elections result in a runoff, Mugabe may lose.[173] Others argue that the election, even if it results in a runoff, will not be free or fair, and that the government will remain unchanged in the short-term. Some have suggested that if Mugabe wins the election, there are members of the ruling party who may be amenable to negotiations with the opposition over the establishment of a transitional government with representation from both parties, to be followed later by general elections. The opposition's role in Zimbabwe's political future may depend on its ability to present a unified and credible alternative to the Mugabe government, as well as its willingness to work with moderate elements of ZANU-PF.

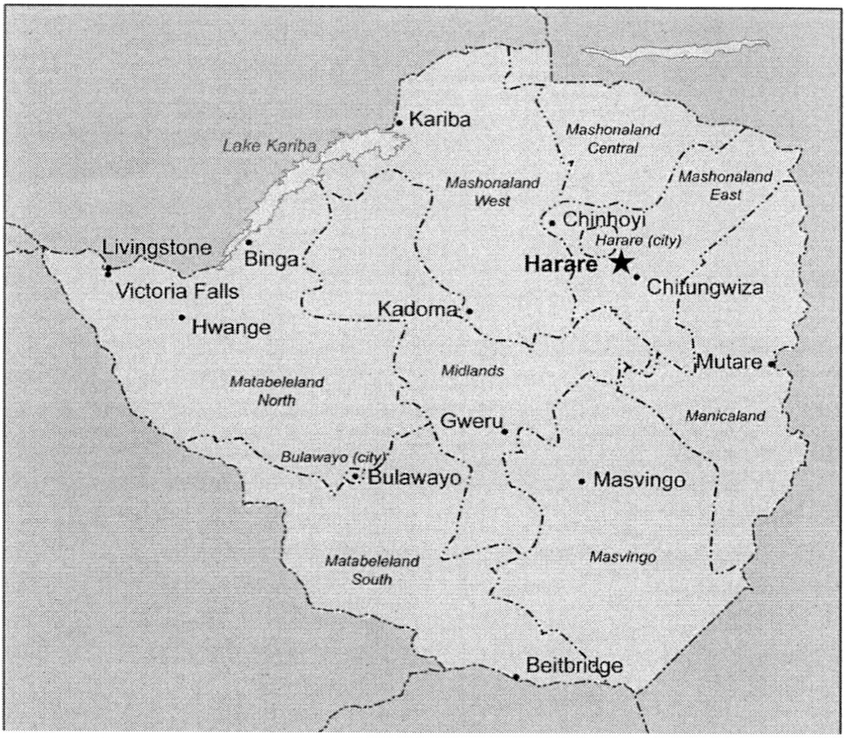

Source: Map Resources. Adapted by CRS. (K.Yancey 11/12/04).

Figure 1. Map of Zimbabwe.

REFERENCES

[1] The Zimbabwe's chief statistician announced in November 2007 that they could no longer calculate the official inflation rate because government price controls have left store shelves largely empty. Some estimate real inflation may be over 100,000%. "Zimbabwe Statistician Says Lack of Goods Hinders Inflation Calculations," *VOA News*, November 28, 2007.

[2] See, for example, Human Rights Watch, *All Over Again: Human Rights Abuses and Flawed Electoral Conditions in Zimbabwe's Coming General Elections,* Vol. 20, No. 2(A), March 2008, and International Crisis Group, "Zimbabwe: Prospects from a Flawed Election," *Africa Report No. 138*, March 20, 2008.

[3] "Zimbabwe 'A Sinking Titanic,'" *Financial Times,* March 22, 2007.

[4] "RSA Parliamentarians Urge Stronger Action Against Zimbabwe," *South African Press Association,* March 28, 2007.

[5] "Zimbabwe Crisis Deepens," *Voice of America*, April 6, 2007.

[6] "Mbeki Rejects Regime Change," *Financial Times,* April 2, 2007.

[7] See, for example, Solidarity Peace Trust, *Destructive Engagement: Violence, Mediation, and Politics in Zimbabwe*, Johannesburg, July 10, 2007.

[8] The government's allegations are outlined in reports produced by the Zimbabwe Republic Police, *Opposition Forces in Zimbabwe: A Trail of Violence* and *Opposition Forces in Zimbabwe: The Naked Truth, Volume 2,*available at [http://www.moha.gov.zw/]. The Zimbabwe Human Rights NGO Forum has refuted the government's claims in *At Best a Falsehood, At Worst, A Lie*, August 2007, available at [http://www.hrforumzim.com].

[9] Press Statement of U.S. Department of State Spokesman Sean McCormack, "Zimbabwe: Civil Society Organization Beatings During President Mbeki's Visit," November 26, 2007.

[10] Barry Bearak, "Zimbabwe Opponent Criticizes Mbeki," *New York Times*, February 14, 2008.

[11] Text of report on Zimbabwean Radio, "Zimbabwe Ruling Party Endorses Mugabe Candidacy for 2008 Elections," *BBC Monitoring,* April 1, 2007.

[12] "Zimbabwe Ruling Party Accused of Manipulating Electoral Process," *Voice of America*, April 18, 2007.

[13] "Mugabe Said Planning to Amend Constitution Over Possible Mid-Term Resignation," *Financial Gazette,* April 13, 2007.

[14] Dumisani Muleya, "Mugabe's Latest Survival Strategy," *Zimbabwe Independent,* April 6, 2007.

[15] See "First Poll Observers in Zimbabwe," *BBC*, March 11, 2008.

[16] "CNN Denied Permission to Cover Elections in Zimbabwe," *CNN*, March 25, 2008.

[17] Lance Guma, "Election Body Calls for More Polling Stations," *SW Radio Africa,* March 11, 2008, available at [http://www.allafrica.com].

[18] This report was originally authored by Raymond W. Copson and Jeffrey Townsend.

[19] For more information on Zimbabwe's land redistribution issue and other historical context, see CRS Report RL3 1229, *Zimbabwe Backgrounder*, by Raymond Copson.

[20] Department for International Development (DFID), *Country Profile: Zimbabwe,* December 2006.

[21] UNAIDS, *Report on the Global AIDS Epidemic 2006*, and CIA, *CIA World Factbook.*

[22] The Washington-based *Foreign Policy* magazine uses 12 economic, social, political, and military indicators to rank countries in order of their "vulnerability to violent internal conflict and social dysfunction." Zimbabwe's ranking on the index dropped 14 points from 2005 to 2006, and another point in 2007 suggesting the country's situation has deteriorated. For more information, see "The Failed States Index," *Foreign Policy*, May/June 2007.

[23] "Imperialists Can't Preach Human Rights," *The Herald,* January 19, 2007.

[24] Jonathan Moyo, former Information Minister, left ZANU-PF and was elected as an independent candidate.

[25] Reporters Without Borders, "No Letup in Abusive Media Tactics Three Weeks Before Legislative Elections," March 8, 2005.

[26] Zimbabwe Human Rights NGO Forum, *Political Violence Report, March 2005.* The forum produces monthly reports on the human rights situation in Zimbabwe and assists victims of violence. See [http://www.hrforumzim.com].

[27] Freedom House, "Country Report: Zimbabwe," *Freedom in the World 2006.*

[28] International Council of Barristers and Advocates, *The State of Justice in Zimbabwe*, December 2004. The Council sent an investigative team to Zimbabwe which included Chairmans of the Bar of England and Wales and the Irish Bar, and Vice Chairman of the South African Bar.

[29] "Zimbabwe Court Rules 2005 Electoral Legislation 'Inconsistent' with Constitution," *The Financial Gazette*, July 27, 2006.

[30] ZESN, *Report on Zimbabwe's 2005 General Election,* April 2005. The ZESN, a coalition of 35 human rights and civic groups based in Zimbabwe, deployed 260 long-term observers and 6000 observers for the election itself.
[31] The report of the ZLHR,a local human rights organization that deployed 44 observers for the election, is available at [http://www.zlhr.org.zw].
[32] "Zimbabwe's Enabler; South Africa Falls Short as Monitor of Democracy," *Washington Post*, April 4, 2005.
[33] "The Real Fraud in Zimbabwe," *Washington Times*, April 6, 2005.
[34] The statement of Secretary Rice, made on April 1, 2005, is available online at [http://www.state.gov/secretary/rm/2005/44 141 .htm].
[35] Secretary-General Annan' s statement is available at [http://www.un.org/News/ossg/].
[36] MISA, *Annual Report, April 2003-March 2004*; "Media Institute Says Press Restrictions in Zimbabwe Rule Out Fair Elections," *Voice Of America (VOA)*, April 5, 2004.
[37] For the text of the POSA, see [http://www.kubatana.net/docs/legisl/posa060203.doc].
[38] Solidarity Peace Trust, *Policing the State*, December 2006.
[39] International Bar Association, "An Analysis of the Zimbabwean Non-Governmental Organizations Bill, 2004," August 24, 2004.
[40] "Title Deeds to 4,000 Farms Nullified," *The Herald,* September 23, 2005.
[41] Human Rights Watch, *All Over Again: Human Rights Abuses and Flawed Electoral Conditions in Zimbabwe's Coming Elections,* Vol. 20, No. 2(A), March 2008.
[42] Media Institute of Southern Africa, "AIPPA, POSA, BSA Amendments Signed into Law," *Media Alert Update*, January 12, 2008.
[43] "Rally Ban a Fatal Govt Assault on Social Contract," *Zimbabwe Independent,* March 2, 2007. The ban was lifted on June 29, 2007.
[44] "Zimbabwe Opposition Leader Taken to Hospital From Court," *CNN,* March 13, 2007, and "Mugabe Foes Vow to Intensify Action," *Washington Post,* March 13, 2007.
[45] "Zimbabwean Police 'Fire-Bombed,'" *BBC*, March 15, 2007.
[46] Statement of U.S. Secretary of State Condoleezza Rice, "Call for Immediate Release of Zimbabwean Opposition Leaders," on March 13, 2007.
[47] Statement issued by the Spokesman of the U.N. Secretary General on March 12, 2007.
[48] "Zimbabwe Leader Faces Growing Condemnation," *Associated Press,* March 15, 2007.

[49] Freedom House, "Country Report: Zimbabwe," *Freedom in the World 2006: The Annual Survey of Political Rights and Civil Liberties.*

[50] DOS, "Zimbabwe," *Country Reports on Human Rights Practices 2007.*

[51] Amnesty International (AI), "Zimbabwe," *Annual Report 2007.*

[52] "Threat by Mugabe," *New York Times*, August 16, 2006.

[53] See Mugabe' s statement in an article from the government-owned newspaper, *The Herald* at "Zimbabwe Press Review for 25 Sep 06", *BBC Monitoring Africa,* September 25, 2006.

[54] "U.N. Slams President Mugabe," *Zimbabwe Independent,* September 29, 2006.

[55] The post of Rapporteur was created by the U.N. Commission on Human Rights in 1985 to investigate questions relating to torture. For information on the Rapporteur' s mandate, see [http://www.ohchr.org/english/issues/torture/rapporteur/index.htm].

[56] Zimbabwe Human Rights NGO Forum, *Political Violence Report, December 2007.*

[57] Zimbabwe Human Rights NGO Forum, *Political Violence Report, December 2006.*

[58] "Zimbabwe Leaders Accused of Abducting Opponents," *New York Times,* March 29, 2007.

[59] Human Rights Watch, *All Over Again: Human Rights Abuses and Flawed Electoral Conditions in Zimbabwe's Coming General Elections,* Vol. 20, No. 2(A), March 2008.

[60] For more information, see the Mission's report at [http://www.icj .org].

[61] The U.N. Special Envoy on Human Settlements Issues in Zimbabwe Anna Kajumulo Tibaijuka, *Report of the Fact-Finding Mission to Zimbabwe to Assess The Scope and Impact of Operation Murambatsvina,* July 2005.

[62] A survey by ActionAid International, a Netherlands-based international development agency, found that 840,000 were directly affected and 1.2 million indirectly affected, while a survey by the independent research firm Afrobarometer reported that an estimated 2.7 million were directly affected.

[63] ActionAid International, *The Impact of Operation Murambatsvina/Restore Order in Zimbabwe,* August 2005.

[64] Tibaijuka, 13.

[65] U.S. Committee for Refugees and Immigrants, "World Refugee Survey, Zimbabwe Country Report," 2003.

[66] DOS, "Zimbabwe," *Country Reports on Human Rights Practices 2005.*

[67] Tibaijuka, 34.

[68] "Clean Up Commendable," *The Herald*, May 23, 2005.

[69] Ibid., 7.
[70] Ibid., 7.
[71] Ibid., 54.
[72] The Secretary-General's statement, made on July 22, 2005, is available online at [http://www.un.org/apps/sg/sgstats.asp?nid= 1589].
[73] See, for example, Zimbabwe Human Rights NGO Forum , "Political Repression Disguised as Civic Mindedness: Operation Murambatsvina One Year Later," November 2006 and *Political Violence Report, October 2007.*
[74] U.N., *United Nations Consolidated Appeals Process (CAP) 2007,* July 2007.
[75] AI, "Zimbabwe: No Justice for the Victims of Forced Evictions," September 2006.
[76] The October 31, 2005 statement is available at [http://www.un.org/News/ossg/].
[77] AI, "Zimbabwe," *Annual Report 2007.*
[78] See the AI report; Solidarity Peace Trust, *Meltdown: Murambatsvina One Year On,* August 30, 2006.
[79] Institute of War and Peace Reporting, "Prosecution of Mugabe Urged," January 20, 2006.
[80] The United States is not party to the Rome Statute. For more information, see CRS Report RL3 1495, *U.S. Policy Regarding the International Criminal Court*, by Jennifer Elsea.
[81] For more information on the "Responsibility to Protect," see the *Report on the International Commission on Intervention and State Sovereignty*, which aims to "reconcil[e] the international community's responsibility to act in the face of massive violations of humanitarian norms while respecting the sovereign rights of states." The report is available at [http://www.iciss.ca/report-en.asp].
[82] The IBA is comprised of Bar Associations and Law Societies around the world. The comments of its Executive Director can be found at [http://www.ibanet.org/iba/article. cfm?article=95].
[83] Tibaijuka, 76.
[84] See an excerpt from South-Africa based website *ZimOnline* in "Ex-Ethiopian Leader Said Behind Zimbabwe's Cleanup Operation," *BBC Monitoring Africa*, February 20, 2006.
[85] For more information on the region's food crisis, see CRS Report RS2 1301, *The Food Crisis in Southern Africa: Background and Issues*, by Charles E. Hanrahan.
[86] United Nations, *2006 CAP Mid-Year Review*, June 2006.

[87] ActionAid International, *The Impact of Operation Murambatsvina/Restore Order in Zimbabwe,* August 2005. This study suggests up to 54% of the country may have become food insecure as a result of Murambatsvina. A more recent USAID study also concluded that Murambatsvina and "more recent evictions " increased vulnerability, according to its "Zimbabwe — Drought and Complex Emergency Situation Report #2," Fiscal Year 2007.

[88] World Food Program, "Zimbabwe: Overview," available at [http://www.wfp.org] and "More Than a Third of Zimbabweans Require Food Assistance," *IRIN*, June 5, 2007.

[89] On the land takeovers in Zimbabwe, see AI, *Zimbabwe: Power and Hunger — Violations of the Right to Food*, October 15, 2004.

[90] "Zimbabwe: The Mother of All Farming Seasons," *IRIN*, October 25, 2007.

[91] Solidarity Peace Trust, *Operation Taguta/Sisuthi*, April 2006.

[92] AI, *Zimbabwe: Power and Hunger.*

[93] "Mugabe Word for Word," *Sky News*, May 24, 2004.

[94] AI, *Zimbabwe: Power and Hunger,* and USAID, *2004 Annual Report for the Office of Foreign Disaster Assistance (OFDA).*

[95] "ZANU-PF Admits Food Crisis," *Institute for War and Peace Reporting* (London), March 7, 2005; "10 More Die of Hunger in Bulawayo," *Zimbabwe Standard*, March 7, 2005; "14 More Die of Hunger in Bulawayo," *Zimbabwe Standard*, February 15, 2005.

[96] "Govt Delays Stall WFP Food Distribution," *Financial Gazette*, December 13, 2006.

[97] Reference to the rulings, made by Judges Nicholas Ndou and Rita Makarau, can be found in DOS, "Zimbabwe," *Country Reports on Human Rights Practices 2005.*

[98] "Zimbabwe Has Highest Percentage of Orphans in the World," *Associated Press*, December 6, 2006.

[99] UNAIDS, *AIDS Epidemic Update,* December 2007.

[100] Dr. Peter Piot, "Launch of the 2005 AIDS Epidemic Update," November 21, 2005. Speech available at [http://data.unaids.org/Media/Speeches02/SP_Piot_EPI05_2 1Nov05_en.pdf].

[101] "Zimbabweans Pledge to Redouble Efforts to Beat AIDS," *VOA,* December 1, 2006. Other figures are more conservative — the United Nations estimates that 10%, or 1 in 10 Zimbabweans, are receiving ART.

[102] Tibaijuka, 40.

[103] Solidarity Peace Trust, *An Account of the Exodus of a Nation's People*, November 2004.

[104] See, for example, Simon Robinson, "Great Leap Backwards," *Time*, May 29, 2005, and the World Bank's "Country Brief" on Zimbabwe, available at [http://www.worldbank.org].
[105] IMF, *Regional Economic Outlook: Sub-Saharan Africa,* September 2006.
[106] "Gono' s Mission Is to Save ZANU-PF, Not the Economy," *LiquidAfrica*, December 3, 2004.
[107] "Country is Committed to Uprooting All Forms of Corruption," *The Herald*, August 24, 2006.
[108] "Much Ado About Money," *IRIN,* August 18, 2006.
[109] "Bag of Bricks: Hyperinflation in Zimbabwe," *The Economist*, August 26, 2006, and "Zimbabwe: Millions no Longer Millionaires," *African Business,* October 2006.
[110] See, for example, "A Zimbabwean Businessman, His Farms Seized, Takes on Mugabe," *Washington Post,* February 24, 2006.
[111] "Mugabe's 82nd Birthday Blast at Zimbabwe," *Business Day*, February 21, 2006.
[112] "In Reversal, Mugabe Seeks White Farmers," *UPI,* December 17, 2006.
[113] "Zimbabwe to Ration Electricity for Homes to Four Hours a Day," *Reuters*, May 10, 2007.
[114] "Power Cuts Halt Harare Factories," *Business Day*, October 29, 2007.
[115] "Zimbabwe Clarifies Nationalization Legislation," *Financial Times*, March 11, 2008.
[116] Zimbabwe is a signatory of the Kimberly Process. For more information, see CRS Report RL30751, *Diamonds and Conflict: Background, Policy, and Legislation,* by Nicolas Cook.
[117] "Zimbabwe: Parliamentary Body Urges State to 'Normalize' Trade Ties with West," *BBC Monitoring Africa*, December 8, 2006.
[118] "Militarization of State Firms Cause for Worry," *Zimbabwe Independent*, May 26, 2006.
[119] "Soldiers Go Hungry," *Financial Gazette*, May 23, 2007.
[120] "Five Accused of Plotting Coup to Topple President," *The Herald,* June 16, 2007.
[121] "Army Investigates Reports of Coup Plot," *SW Radio Africa*, June 14, 2007.
[122] "Rice Targets 6 'Outposts of Tyranny,'" *Washington Times*, January 19, 2005. The others were Cuba, Burma, North Korea, Iran, and Belarus.
[123] "Zimbabwe's Mugabe Lashes Out at Rice, Blair at Campaign Launch," *AFP*, February 11, 2005.

[124] DOS, "Zimbabwe a Textbook Case of Bad Governance, U.S. Official Says," February 28, 2005.
[125] For information on human trafficking and related legislation, see CRS Report RL30545, *Trafficking in Persons: The U.S. and International Response*, by Clare Ribando.
[126] A Tier 2 rating means that the government still does not meet the minimum standards for the elimination of trafficking, but is making significant efforts to do so. For more information, see U.S. Department of State, *Trafficking in Persons Report 2007,* available at [http://www.state.gov/g/tip/rls/tiprpt/2007/].
[127] Seventy-seven individuals are named in the executive order (EO 13288), but one of these, Vice President Simon Muzenda, has died.
[128] The text of this annex to EO 13288 can be found at [http://www.whitehouse.gov].
[129] "Bush Backs Mbeki on Zimbabwe," *The Guardian* (London) July 10, 2003.
[130] "US Seeks 'Coalition' to Force Zimbabwe Regime Change," *The Independent* (UK), August 25, 2004.
[131] Department of State, FY2008 Foreign Operations Congressional Budget Justification.
[132] DOS's *Consular Information Sheet* for Zimbabwe is available at [http://travel.state.gov/].
[133] "EU Demands Probe into Congress of Trade Union Attacks," *Zimbabwe Standard,* September 24, 2006.
[134] "Zimbabwe's Mugabe Marks 81st Birthday With Attack on Opposition, Blair," *AFP*, February 26, 2005.
[135] "France, US Say 'No Zimbabwe-UK Dispute, Call for Internal Dialogue," *BBC Monitoring Africa,* July 21, 2006.
[136] "Commonwealth Observer Group's Preliminary Report on Zimbabwean Presidential Elections," March 14, 2002. Available at [http://www.afrol.com].
[137] "Mugabe Rules Out Zimbabwe's Return to the Commonwealth," *AFP*, December 16, 2003.
[138] "Beijing Quietly Cools Relations With Mugabe," *Financial Times*, June 5, 2007.
[139] Defense analysts describe the K-8 as a trainer jet with light ground attack capabilities. Zambia and Namibia have likewise purchased K-8s from China.
[140] EIU, "The Government is to Buy More Jets from China," September 15, 2006.

[141] Excerpt from South Africa-based website *ZimOnline* in "Zimbabwe Leader 'Frantically' Seeking Allies," *BBC Monitoring Africa*, November 23, 2006.
[142] "China Aid 'Snub' to Enable South Africa to Extract Concessions from Zimbabwe," *BBC Monitoring Africa,* August 1, 2005.
[143] "Zimbabwe, China to Negotiate $2 Billion Dollar Loan Deal," *AFP*, December 22, 2006 and China and "Beijing Cools on Mugabe China in Africa," *International Herald Tribune*, May 4, 2007.
[144] "Chinese Envoy Supports Zimbabwe's Land Reforms," *AFP*, November 2, 2004.
[145] "Iran Slams Sactions Against Zim," *AllAfrica,* November 22, 2006.
[146] See CRS Report RS2 1353, *New Partnership for Africa's Development (NEPAD),* by Nicolas Cook.
[147] September "Nigeria Rolls Out Red Carpet for Tsvangirai," *Zimbabwe Standard*, November 15, 2004.
[148] "The SA, Nigeria, and MDC Connection," *The Herald,* November 6, 2005.
[149] "Hotfoot from Harare," *Africa Confidential*, Vol. 48, No. 24, November 30, 2007.
[150] Michael Wines, "Influx from Zimbabwe to South Africa Tests Both," *New York Times*, June 22, 2007.
[151] "Zimbabwe Pays Part of IMF Debt," *Washington Post,* September 2, 2005.
[152] "We Are Not Quiet Diplomats," *Daily Mail and Guardian* (Johannesburg), November 5, 2004.
[153] "South Africa Ends 's 'Silence' on Zimbabwe, Urges Harare 'to Respect Rule of Law,'" *BBC Monitoring Africa*, March 14, 2007.
[154] ICG, *Zimbabwe: Another Election Chance*, 14.
[155] "Tsvangirai Changes Tune on Mbeki' s Quiet Diplomacy," *Business Day*, October 29, 2004.
[156] "Mbeki Pays Tribute to Zimbabwe, Says Polls Will Be Free and Fair," *AFP*, March 2, 2005.
[157] "Mbeki Criticizes U.S Over Zimbabwe," *BBC*, February 22, 2005.
[158] For more information on challenges to a possible Zuma presidency, see CRS Report RL3 1697, *South Africa: Current Issues and U.S. Relations,* by Lauren Ploch.
[159] "I'm No Mugabe, but I Have Sympathy for What He Has Done," *The Sunday Telegraph* (London), November 26, 2006.
[160] "Chorus of Disapproval Grows As Sexwale Speaks Out on Mugabe," *Zimbabwe Independent*, October 6, 2006.
[161] "Zimbabwe 'Ignoring' SA Diplomacy," *BBC*, May 15, 2007.

[162] "AU Report Slams Erosion of Rule of Law," *Zimbabwe Independent*, July 16, 2004.

[163] "It's the Very Leaders Who Are Denying the People Their Justice," *Financial Gazette,* July 20, 2006.

[164] "African Union Slams Human Rights Record," *IRIN,* January 3, 2006.

[165] International Press Institute, "IPI Disappointed By African Union's Slow Progress in Criticizing Zimbabwe's Record on Human Rights, Press Freedom," April 4, 2006. IPI is a global network of editors, media executives and leading journalists in over 110 countries that promotes press freedoms and journalistic standards.

[166] "Mkapa Has a Long Shot at Moving 'Bad Boy' Mugabe," *AllAfrica*, August 25, 2006.

[167] For further information on the APRM and NEPAD, see CRS Report RS21353, *New Partnership for Africa's Development (NEPAD)*, by Nicolas Cook.

[168] "Harare Raps African Union Human Rights Body," *U.S. Fed News*, July 6, 2005.

[169] *SADC Principles and Guidelines Governing Democratic Elections* (Adopted by the SADC Summit, Mauritius, August 2004). Available at [http://www.iss.co.za].

[170] ICG, *Zimbabwe: Another Election Chance*, 13.

[171] Teddy Brett and Simon Winter, "Origins of the Zimbabwe Crisis," *Focus* (Helen Suzman Foundation), June 2003.

[172] "Zimbabwe Army's Deserters Underscore Country's Economic Troubles," *Christian Science Monitor,* April 25, 2007.

[173] Barry Bearak, "In Crisis, Zimbabwe Asks: Could Mugabe Lose?" *New York Times*, March 7, 2008.

In: Focus on Zimbabwe
Editor: Alfred J. Cartage, pp. 55-86
ISBN: 978-1-60692-186-9

Chapter 2

ZIMBABWE: 2008 ELECTIONS AND IMPLICATIONS FOR U.S. POLICY*

Lauren Ploch
Analyst in African Affairs
Foreign Affairs, Defense, and Trade Division

ABSTRACT

On March 29, 2008, Zimbabwe held presidential, parliamentary and local elections. More than a month later, the country's political future remains uncertain. For the first time since independence, the ruling party has lost its majority in the National Assembly. After a month of rising tensions, the results of the presidential race were belatedly announced on May 2. They indicated that opposition leader Morgan Tsvangirai had received more votes than the incumbent, President Robert Mugabe, but had failed to garner the 50 percent needed to avoid a runoff.

Reports of violence and political repression have increased significantly since the elections, which were held amidst a deepening economic crisis in the Southern African country. Zimbabwe's gross domestic product (GDP) has decreased over 40 percent in the last decade, the inflation rate is estimated at over 165,000 percent, and unemployment is higher than 80 percent. The adult HIV infection rate of 20 percent has contributed to a sharp drop in life expectancy, and more than a third of the population is expected to require food aid in 2008. Deteriorating conditions in the country have led many Zimbabweans to

* Excerpted from CRS Report Order Code RL34509, dated May 22, 2008.

emigrate to neighboring countries, creating a substantial burden on the region. In South Africa, Zimbabwean immigrants and others have recently been the target of xenophobic attacks.

President Mugabe's government is seen as autocratic and repressive by its critics, and its human rights record is poor. The regime has suppressed freedom of speech and assembly, and many contend that it restricts access to food, already scarce, in opposition areas. Many regional and international observers suggest the presidential runoff, which the government has postponed until June 27, should not be held amidst the current level of political violence. The U.S. Secretary of State has labeled Zimbabwe an "outpost of tyranny," and other Administration officials have accused the ruling party of rigging the election and orchestrating the current violence. The United States has enforced targeted sanctions against top Zimbabwe officials and associates since 2002. Congress has expressed its opposition to the government's undemocratic policies in the Zimbabwe Democracy and Economic Recovery Act of 200 1(P.L. 107-99) and other subsequent legislation, including H.Con.Res. 100, S.Con.Res. 25, S. 1500, S.Res. 533, and H.Res. 1230 during the 1 10th Congress. For more background, see CRS Report RL32723, *Zimbabwe*.

President Robert Mugabe, 84, and his party, the Zimbabwe African National Union - Patriotic Front (ZANU-PF), have ruled Zimbabwe since its independence in 1980. Rising inflation and unemployment rates contributed in the late 1990s to the creation of the opposition Movement for Democratic Change (MDC). The MDC enjoyed initial success, campaigning against a referendum in 2000 that would have expanded the president's powers, made government officials immune from prosecution, and allowed the uncompensated seizure of white-owned land for redistribution to black farmers. The referendum failed, and the MDC won nearly half the parliamentary seats in that year's election. ZANU-PF has since taken numerous, often undemocratic actions to maintain power.

Following the violent March 2007 assault by police on government critics, which drew widespread international criticism, South African President Thabo Mbeki initiated a mediation effort between the Government of Zimbabwe and the opposition. The main objective of the mediation, as described by Mbeki, was to create political conditions for free and fair elections, the results of which would be accepted by all parties. Although the negotiations resulted in the amendment of some laws seen as restricting press freedom and political activity, the talks were abandoned after Mugabe announced that elections would be held on March 29, 2008.[1] Human rights activists argue that the legislative changes were cosmetic and that the talks failed to create a level playing field prior to the elections.[2]

March 2008 Elections

Election Preparations

Many domestic and international observers assert that elections since 2000 have fallen short of democratic standards. In the period preceding the March 2008 elections, civil society activists reported significant preelection irregularities. Critics charged that the Zimbabwe Election Commission (ZEC), which oversees elections, lacked independence, and that it was further crippled by limited administrative capacity and budget shortages.[3] The electoral body is led by Justice George Chiweshe, a former military officer, and reports indicate that the Commission and its regional offices are staffed by numerous former military personnel. Reports from domestic groups suggest that the registration process was, at best, inconsistent, and there is no indication that the ZEC addressed alleged inaccuracies in the voters' roll from previous elections. On the eve of the election, the MDC accused the government of printing nine million ballots, even though there were only 5.9 million registered voters.[4]

The March elections were Zimbabwe's first attempt at holding "harmonized" elections for all levels of government (local, National Assembly, Senate, and presidential) simultaneously. In addition to the logistical challenges this posed, civic groups argued that the complexity of a four-ballot election required a nationwide voter education campaign. They claim that the ZEC' s education efforts were inadequate and that independent non-governmental organizations (NGOs) were barred from engaging in voter education programs of their own.

The Zimbabwe Election Support Network (ZESN), a domestic observer group composed of 38 NGOs, alleges that the ruling party had redrawn constituencies[5] to ensure its continued hold on power. In its pre-election report, ZESN argued that there were not enough polling stations designated for urban areas, where the opposition is believed to have its strongest support. ZESN' s report also suggested that, as in past elections, the ruling party manipulated state resources for campaign purposes.[6] And despite amendments to two laws, the Public Order and Security Act (POSA) and the Access to Information and Protection of Privacy Act (AIPPA), which critics suggest restrict freedom of speech and assembly, advocacy groups argue that the police selectively interpreted the laws and significantly limited the MDC' s ability to campaign.[7] Sections of POSA which prohibit false statements "prejudicial" to the state and criminalize statements construed as engendering hostility toward the president remain in effect.

Alleged Vote Buying

In addition to the allegedly partisan administration of the elections, many observers allege that the government used public resources to buy votes. In the weeks preceding the polls, President Mugabe announced significant salary increases for the military and civil servants and signed into law the Indigenisation and Economic Empowerment Bill, requiring foreign-owned firms to transfer 51 percent of their shares to domestic investors. His administration also reportedly distributed vehicles and agricultural equipment worth millions of U.S. dollars to ZANU-PF supporters.[8] At the same time, in a country where 45 percent of the population is considered by the World Food Program to be malnourished, domestic groups reported numerous incidents of opposition supporters being denied access to state food supplies.[9]

Pre-Election Violence

According to a domestic human rights group, the year prior the 2008 elections was marked by a significant increase in incidents of politically motivated violence from previous years. In 2007, there were 603 reported incidents of torture, 865 incidents of assault, and 2,766 reports of arrest and detention. In the months directly preceding the elections, from November 2007 to March 2008, there were 1775 reported incidents of political violence.[10] The government routinely deployed riot police to break up demonstrations, meetings and rallies, despite changes to the laws regulating freedom of assembly. In January, police allegedly teargassed and assaulted protestors in Harare after a local magistrate overruled a police order banning the march.[11] In February, members of the Progressive Teachers Union of Zimbabwe reported being abducted and beaten by ZANU-PF supporters; according to their accounts several members of the police and intelligence service were present during the attacks.[12] According to reports, the perpetrators were not arrested, but the union leaders were charged with violating a law that prohibits the distribution of pamphlets in public areas.[13]

Several of the country's security service chiefs, including the heads of the army and the police, have publicly announced that they would not recognize an electoral victory by anyone other that Mugabe.[14] In speeches and statements to the press, they and other public officials, including the President himself, have referred to opposition leaders as traitors, political witches, and puppets or agents of the West. In October 2007, the International Bar Association issued a report accusing Zimbabwe's police of being "blatantly partisan" and suggesting that the force's failure to guarantee equal protection of the law "is a major obstacle to democracy in Zimbabwe and a considerable impediment to free and fair elections."[15] As part of the January 2008 electoral reforms, police were banned from the polling stations to allay fears of intimidation. However, just over a week before the elections President Mugabe issued a decree allowing police into polling stations, allegedly to help disabled voters.

Election Monitoring

The Government of Zimbabwe reportedly invited election observers from over 40 countries and regional organizations, including the Southern African Development Community (SADC) and the African Union (AU), but barred observers from countries considered to be critical of its policies.[16] CNN and other western media organizations and journalists were reportedly denied permission to cover the elections.[17] The AU observer mission, led by former President of Sierra Leone Tejan Kabbah, issued a preliminary statement after the elections suggesting that the elections were generally free and fair and expressed the will of the people. Kabbah urged all parties to accept the results. The SADC observer mission found the elections to be "a credible expression of the will of the people" but noted concerns regarding opposition access to the media, inflammatory statements by senior security officials, the presence of police officers at polling stations, and the delay in the publication of the voters' roll. Two members of the delegation, both from South Africa's largest opposition party, refused to sign the report, calling the elections "chaotic" and "deeply flawed."[18] Other observer groups differed with the SADC findings. The delegation of the World Council of Churches, in a joint statement with the African Council of Churches, found the elections to be "skewed in favor of the incumbent who openly utilized state resources to his advantage" and reported media bias, "violence, intimidation and outright confrontation," and the use of food as a "political tool."[19]

Press Restrictions

Two international journalists, one a Pulitzer Prizewinning American correspondent for the *New York Times*, were arrested on April 3, 2008. After several days in jail, they were released on bail but were blocked from leaving the country. They were acquitted on April 16. Several other journalists, both domestic and foreign, have been arrested since the elections. The director of the ZESN was briefly detained by police on April 14 and questioned about possible ties to the Washington-based National Democratic Institute, which monitors elections worldwide. More recently, the editor of *The Standard*, the country's only remaining independent newspaper, was arrested on May 5 for printing an editorial by opposition leader Arthur Mutambara entitled, "A Shameful Betrayal of National Independence." He was later released, but faces trial for publishing statements prejudicial to the state.

ELECTION RESULTS

Parliament

The MDC, which split into two factions in 2005 (known as MDC-T and MDC-M for their respective leaders, Morgan Tsvangirai and Arthur Mutambara), remained divided for the March elections, and this division likely cost the party several parliamentary seats.[20] The ZEC, widely criticized for its delayed release of the electoral results, announced the National Assembly results four days after the election. The MDC factions, which reunited on April 28, won a majority in the 220-seat National Assembly with 109 seats, over ZANU-PF's 97.[21] Three weeks after the election, the electoral commission conducted a recount of 23 of these races, an overwhelming majority of which were won by the opposition.[22] The original results were upheld. On April 6, the ZEC announced that the ruling party had retained its majority in the Senate, where over one-third of its 93 members are appointed by the president. Of the 60 seats directly elected, ZANU-PF won 30, MDC-Tsvangirai 24, and MDC-Mutambara 6. Several senior ruling party members lost their parliamentary seats, including the Ministers of Justice, Agriculture, Mines, Energy, and Transport, and several senior MDC-M parliamentarians, including Mutambara, lost to MDC-T candidates.

The Presidency

The MDC's decision to contest the election while still divided may also have cost the party a clear victory in the presidential race. In February 2008, then-ZANU-PF senior member Simba Makoni announced his intention to run against President Mugabe in the upcoming elections.[23] He was subsequently expelled from the party and ran as an independent, although he was rumored to have been supported by several senior ruling party officials. MDC faction leader Arthur

Mutambara, who had planned to run against Mugabe and Tsvangirai, withdrew as a presidential candidate and expressed his support for Makoni. It is unclear how many supporters of his faction voted for Makoni instead of Tsvangirai.

The main MDC faction claimed victory for Tsvangirai days after the election with over 50 percent of the votes cast, basing its claim on tallies of poll results posted outside the polling stations and constituency centers immediately following the elections. Some have differed with the MDC count, suggesting that while Tsvangirai almost certainly received more votes than Mugabe, he may not have achieved the necessary 50 percent to avoid a runoff.[24] ZESN has noted that results were not posted in three constituency tabulation centers despite a legal requirement to do so.

The results of the presidential race were not officially announced until five weeks after the elections. The opposition called for a nationwide strike on April 14 to protest the delayed release of results, asking supporters to stay home rather than to demonstrate publicly. Dozens of opposition supporters, including a newly elected member of parliament, were reportedly arrested that day for allegedly trying to incite violence or for obstructing the freedom of movement. According to reports, the strike was largely unsuccessful. With over 80 percent unemployment, some analysts suggest many Zimbabweans could not afford to miss a day's wages; other Zimbabweans said they had not heard of the strike.[25] On the evening of May 2, the ZEC declared that Tsvangirai had received 47.9 percent of the votes, while Mugabe received 43.2 percent and Makoni 8.3 percent. Some in the international community questioned whether the government's delay in releasing the presidential results should be considered a political coup. The MDC appealed unsuccessfully to the courts to have the results released, but the electoral commission claimed that it could not do so until a "process of verification of the presidential ballots" was complete.[26]

Runoff Elections Called

Although the opposition accuses the government of manipulating the presidential results and initially objected to participating in a runoff, Morgan Tsvangirai has agreed to stand against President Mugabe in a second round of voting. The MDC has suggested that the government had access to the ballot boxes for over two weeks in April without opposition or observer supervision, and thus they could not be sure the ballots had not been tampered with. ZESN has also questioned the validity of the presidential results, saying, "ZESN cannot substantiate ZEC figures as the network is not aware of the chain of custody of the ballot materials during the aforementioned period" and claiming that the delayed announcement of the presidential results undermined the impartiality of the ZEC. These concerns have also been echoed by the United States and others.

Having waited for over a month to hear the final results from the first round of elections, it appears Zimbabweans will have another delay before the second round. While the electoral law requires the government to hold a runoff election within 21 days of announcing the initial results, the ZEC has declared that the runoff will not be held until June 27, three months after the first round. Some analysts have questioned whether Zimbabwe's government can afford another election, estimated to cost up to $60 million. According to official Reserve Bank figures, government borrowing in the first three months of 2008 was 43 percent above the projected budget deficit for the year.[27]

The MDC initially called for the immediate deployment of election observers from outside Africa (in addition to the SADC and AU observers) as well as the deployment of regional peacekeepers during the runoff. The party has since modified its demands and suggests that an increased SADC and AU observer presence will be sufficient, if combined with an immediate repeal of restrictions on the MDC' s ability to campaign and an end to political violence. The opposition remains largely unable to hold public rallies, which were banned by police in the capital in mid-April. MDC supporters now await the return of Tsvangirai, who has been outside the country since the elections. The party has expressed concerns about his safety and, given post-election statements by government officials accusing Tsvangirai of treason, some believe he will not be allowed to campaign freely inside the country.[28] The opposition leader was tried, and acquitted, for treason in 2004. Many observers also remain skeptical that the government will publish the second round results in a timely manner, given the significant first round delay. Based on interviews with high-ranking Zimbabwean officials, the International Crisis Group (ICG) suggests that if the runoff results in a Tsvangirai victory, a military coup will result.[29]

Coalition Government?

Zimbabwe's state-controlled media has sent mixed signals about the regime's post-election plans. On April 23, the government-owned *Herald* newspaper printed an editorial that suggested SADC should mediate between the parties to create a transitional coalition government, led by President Mugabe, that would organize new elections.[30] The following day the paper announced on its website that a unity government was "not feasible." The head of South Africa's ruling party has called discussions of a unity government one "appropriate" option.[31] According to the

ICG' s sources, some senior ZANU-PF members, including Vice President Joyce Mujuru and Reserve Bank governor Gideon Gono, tried to convince the president to accept a unity government, but were overruled by senior security officials. Critics allege that the ruling party may try to exercise influence over the courts to overturn the MDC's parliamentary majority. Both parties have challenged the results of over 50 parliamentary races, and although the new parliament can be sworn in during the review, the judiciary's findings could affect the balance of power in the parliament. Central to ZANU-PF concerns, its critics assert, are questions regarding immunity for serious human rights abuses committed since independence.

Both domestic and international observers have expressed concerns that rising violence in Zimbabwe has contributed to a climate of fear and intimidation that may inhibit voters from participating in a runoff election. The lead South African delegate in SADC's observer mission, Ambassador Kingsley Mamabolo, has suggested that the current political climate is too violent for a runoff, saying "You cannot have the next round taking place in this atmosphere; it will not be helpful."[32] The observer mission had been tasked by President Mbeki with investigating allegations of violence, and is expected to produce recommendations to the South African president on how to alleviate tensions. On May 14, SADC's Executive Secretary repeated Mamabolo's findings, "At the moment we can't say the playing ground is safe or will be fair."[33] SADC and the AU have announced a significant increase in the number of poll observers for the runoff.

Post-Election Violence

Although observers suggest that election day was largely peaceful, reports of politically-motivated violence have since increased to a level not seen in two decades, according to advocacy groups. Human Rights Watch has called the reports of violence "a brutal campaign of torture and intimidation" and has documented direct involvement by Zimbabwe's security forces and its officers.[34] The Zimbabwe Association of Doctors for Human Rights has reported that its doctors have treated hundreds of victims with injuries consistent with assault and torture since the election date, and that "the violence is now on such a scale that it is impossible to properly document all cases."[35] The MDC alleges that over 40 of its supporters have been killed. U.S. Ambassador James McGee has implicated the ruling party in orchestrating the attacks (see *U.S. Policy* below).[36]

ZANU-PF and the Zimbabwean army have denied involvement with the attacks, although the army, police, intelligence service, "war veterans"[37] and Zimbabwe's National Youth Service, also known as the "Green Bombers," have all been implicated. One week after the elections, self-styled war veteran leader Jabuli Sibanda warned, "It has come to our realization that the elections were used as another war front to prepare for the re-invasion of our country.... As freedom fighters, we feel compelled to repel the invasion," echoing a frequent Mugabe refrain that an opposition victory would be tantamount to the British reinstating colonial rule. The state-owned *Herald* newspaper, contributed to fears of a white takeover in the wake of the election, reporting, "An increasing number of white former commercial farmers are reportedly threatening resettled black farmers throughout the country with eviction from their farms or face the wrath of an anticipated 'incoming MDC government.'"[38] These pronouncements coincided with farm invasions throughout the country, and by April 16 the Commercial Farmers Union reported that over 100 of the estimated remaining 400 white farmers had been forced off their lands.

Since independence, Mugabe' s regime has employed terminology associated with military-style campaigns for government programs ranging from the implementation of price controls, known as Operation Reduce Prices, to the demolition of informal urban settlements, or Operation *Murambatsvina* (translated as "Clean Out the Filth").[39] Reports suggest that the recent round of violence has its own campaign name, Operation *Mavhoterapapi* ("Who did you vote for?").[40] Critics note the government's historic use of violent tactics against political opponents, pointing to the infamous Operation *Gukurahundi* ("The rain that washes away the chaff before the rain"), the violent "pacification" campaign by a North Korean- trained military unit, the 5th Brigade, in the 1980s against alleged dissidents and supporters of ZANU-PF's political rival at the time, the Zimbabwe African People's Union (ZAPU). *Gukurahundi* is now better known as the Matabeleland Massacres, which resulted in the deaths of as many as 20,000 civilians, mostly from the Ndebele ethnic group in the southwest.[41] That 5th Brigade was led by then-Lt. Col. Perence Shire, now commander of Zimbabwe's Air Force. Other security officials involved in the campaign now hold senior government posts, including Defense Minister Sydney Sekeremayi and Rural Housing Minister Emerson Mnangagwa. Mnangagwa, then Minister of State Security in charge of intelligence, once reportedly warned that the government would burn down "all the villages infested with dissidents." He has been considered a possible successor to Mugabe within the party and is rumored to be in charge of Joint Operations Command (JOC), a secretive group of the country's security chiefs and top commanders, that some allege now control the government.[42]

Zimbabwe's rural areas appear to be the hardest hit by the violence; the U.S. Embassy in Harare has documented thousands who have fled the countryside for urban areas. Most Harare medical clinics are at full capacity, according to the U.S.

Agency for International Development (USAID).[43] Zimbabwe's largest farmers' union reports that militias have displaced 40,000 farm workers, and there are widespread reports of burned homes, granaries, and livestock.[44] Human Rights Watch has detailed the "re-education" and torture of more than 70 MDC supporters, seven of whom reportedly died from their injuries, in Mashonaland province on May 5.[45] Amnesty International reports that victims are often denied medical access and that humanitarian organizations have been targeted by militias for providing assistance.[46] The United Nations' resident representative in Zimbabwe has warned of an impending crisis, stating, "there is an emerging pattern of political violence inflicted mainly, but not exclusively, on suspected followers of the MDC." The level of violence was confirmed by an 8-person SADC mission, "we have seen it, there are people in hospital who said they have been tortured, you have seen pictures, you have seen pictures of houses that have been destroyed and so on."[47]

Some who have fled to the cities have faced further intimidation. On April 25, police raided the MDC's Harare office, arresting some 200 people, many of whom were reportedly supporters who had suffered attacks in their rural homes. Of those arrested, 29 were released that day, the majority were released four days later. Police also raided the office of the domestic observation group, ZESN. In both raids the police, allegedly looking for subversive documents, took computers and documents. On May 9, police arrested the leaders of the Zimbabwe Congress of Trade Unions (ZCTU) based on speeches made at a worker's day rally. The head of the Progressive Teacher's Union has also been arrested. On May 5, more than 50 Zimbabweans were reportedly beaten by riot police during a public protest against the ongoing violence in the city of Bulawayo; eleven members of a women's advocacy group were arrested.

Some Zimbabwean officials, including the country's police chief, have accused the opposition of rigging and inciting violence. According to press reports, over 100 election officers have arrested since the elections on charges of committing fraud and abusing public office in favor of the MDC, at least five have been convicted.[48] Independent reports suggest that teachers, who held many of the election officer positions, have been targeted by government supporters. There are rumors that so-called "war veterans" will be disguised as police in polling places during the runoff to intimidate voters.[49]

Table 1. Regional Efforts to Block Arms Transfer to Zimbabwe

On April 18, 2008, as the Chinese freighter *An Yue Jiang* sat in the waters off South Africa's port city of Durban waiting to unload its cargo, the High Court of South Africa issued a court order blocking the cargo's transfer through South African territory.[50] According to court documents, the ship carried 77 tons of bullets, rocket- propelled grenades, and mortars bound for Zimbabwe. Freight and dock workers of the South African Transport and Allied Workers Union (SATAWU) had already refused to unload or transport the shipment. Their protest was backed by the powerful Congress of Southern African Trade Unions (COSATU) and International Transport Workers' Federation (ITF), which called for an international boycott of the vessel, dubbed by some as the "Ship of Shame." The unions based their protest on concerns that the weapons could fuel violence in the aftermath of Zimbabwe's elections. The international media closely tracked the freighter's location as it searched for another African port in which to unload the cargo. Zambia's President publicly urged regional governments to bar the *An Yue Jiang* from entering their waters. He welcomed Mozambique's decision not to allow the ship access, "because we don't want a situation which will escalate the (tension) in Zimbabwe more than what it is." U.S. Assistant Secretary of State Jendayi Frazer called upon both the regional governments and China to prevent the weapons transfer. On April 22, a Chinese Foreign Ministry spokesperson announced that the ship would return to China. The *An Yue Jiang* later docked in Angola to refuel and unload construction supplies bound for the Angolan market, but was denied permission to unload its Zimbabwe cargo.

INTERNATIONAL REACTIONS

The international community has been divided over how to respond to the current political impasse in Zimbabwe. As the weeks progressed after the elections without the announcement of official results, world leaders began to debate whether Zimbabwe was "in crisis."[51] MDC leader Morgan Tsvangirai traveled throughout the region to advocate for intervention. The African Union joined the growing number of calls for the release of the election results on April 20. As the delay continued, media attention turned to focus on a Chinese arms shipment bound for Zimbabwe. In an April 23 speech to the House of Commons, British Prime Minister Gordon Brown called for an international arms embargo against Zimbabwe, accusing the government of rigging the elections and calling the political situation "completely unacceptable."[52] The European Union (EU) maintains targeted sanctions against members of Mugabe's administration, and EU sanctions already prohibit member states from selling weapons to the country. The United States, which also prohibits weapons sales to Zimbabwe and maintains targeted sanctions, has expressed support for Brown's proposal.

The Southern African Development Community (SADC)

Zambia's President, Levy Mwanawasa, who is also head of the regional body SADC, convened an extraordinary one-day meeting of the Southern African heads of state on April 12, 2008 to discuss Zimbabwe's elections. SADC has remained largely silent in recent years as Zimbabwe's political and economic crisis has worsened. Mwanawasa, however, expressed public concern with the situation in Zimbabwe in 2007, calling the country "a sinking Titanic whose passengers are jumping out to save their lives."[53] He convened a similar emergency summit in late March 2007, following the beating and arrest of opposition officials earlier that month. Although the SADC leaders reportedly chastised President Mugabe privately at that time, they did not publicly condemn the regime's actions and instead appointed South Africa's President Mbeki to mediate between the Zimbabwean government and the opposition.

During the April 12 summit, attended by Tsvangirai and Makoni but not Mugabe, the SADC leaders declined to call the situation in Zimbabwe a crisis. They did, however, publicly urge the government to release the electoral results "expeditiously," allow opposition representatives to be present when vote tabulations were verified, and ensure that a runoff, if needed, would be held in a "secure environment." The SADC leaders also called on Mbeki to continue his role as mediator.[54] According to some reports, Mwanawasa asked the leaders to seek solutions that would allow "the people's verdict" to be heard so that Zimbabweans could "turn [over] a new leaf in their history." Zimbabwe civil society groups have been supportive of SADC' s statements on the electoral results, but critical of its continued support for Mbeki's mediation. Mugabe reportedly called the SADC meeting "a show staged by Britain."[55]

The African Union (AU)

In a communique on April 17, the African Union expressed concern over the delayed results, "which creates an atmosphere of tension that is not in the least conducive to the consolidation of the democratic process that was so felicitously launched through the organization of the elections."[56] In early May, Chairman of the AU Commission Jean Ping led an AU mission to Zimbabwe, Zambia, and South Africa. He called for Zimbabwe's political actors to:

> to conduct their activities in a free, transparent, tolerant, and non-violent manner to enable eligible Zimbabweans [to] exercise their democratic rights. It is essential also that peace and security be maintained, and that the will of the people be respected by all stakeholders once the results are announced.[57]

While the AU has traditionally deferred to regional mediation efforts, reports suggest the AU Chairman, Tanzanian President Jakaya Kikwete (who is also a member of SADC), may be considering calls to widen the Mbeki-led SADC mediation and encourage a greater role by the United Nations. Kenya's new prime minister, Raila Odinga, and former U.N. Secretary-General Kofi Annan have commented that Southern African leaders could do more to resolve the crisis. Senegalese President Abdoulaye Wade has called for the AU to oversee the second round of elections. Zimbabwe's state media reports that the government has rejected AU and SADC plans to expand their monitoring teams for the runoff and that only the individuals who had been invited to monitor the first round would be allowed to cover the second.[58]

It remains unclear what steps the African Union may take if its observers were to find the runoff election lacking in credibility. The African Union has some precedent for intervening in support of democracy within its member countries, should it chose to do so.[59] The intervention of AU leaders in the early days of the 2007/2008 Kenyan election crisis is viewed by many as having helped move the two opposed parties toward negotiations and an eventual post-election agreement. Some analysts suggest that if they were to play a similar role in Zimbabwe, it could diffuse the level of political violence, and might allow members of the ruling party who are rumored to support a transition to play a more open role in discussions about a possible coalition government. As in Kenya, however, negotiations toward any sort of transition, or even a power-sharing arrangement, are likely to be extremely challenging, given that they are expected to have to address immunity issues for Mugabe and his security officials. But diplomatic pressure, even from regional leaders, may have a limited effect on the Zimbabwean government. There have been reports that President Mugabe has refused to take calls from the AU leadership, including President Kikwete. Some, including the MDC and South Africa's opposition, have called for the African Union to send a peacekeeping force to Zimbabwe.

South Africa

President Thabo Mbeki has been the target of growing criticism from opposition parties, trade unions, and civil society groups for his reaction to Zimbabwe's elections. Mbeki, after visiting Mugabe in Harare on his way to the April 12 SADC summit, declared he did not believe Zimbabwe was facing a crisis, that the delayed release of the presidential results was a "natural process," and that Zimbabweans must patiently await their release. Tsvangirai has criticized Mbeki for his "quiet support for the dictatorship."[60]

Others within the South African government and its ruling party appear to take a harder line on the Zimbabwe issue than Mbeki. "In resolving the problem of Zimbabwe, Thabo Mbeki is not speaking on behalf of the ANC," a spokesman for the ruling African National Congress youth wing declared in April.[61] The new president of the ANC, Jacob Zuma, who defeated Mbeki in December 2007 for the party presidency, openly criticized the delayed announcement of the results, saying, "There is a crisis in Zimbabwe. We ought to stand up and do something about it." While not directly charging the Mugabe administration with rigging, he has distanced himself from Mbeki's "quiet diplomacy" approach. In late April, he told reporters, "Definitely there is something wrong with those elections.... I think the manner in which the electoral commission has acted has discredited itself, and therefore that is tantamount to sabotaging the elections."[62] While he has not called for Mbeki to step down as mediator, Zuma has said "I imagine that the leaders in Africa should really move in to unlock this logjam,"[63] and called for African leaders to "assist" Mbeki as mediator, "given the gravity of the situation."[64] The new speaker of the parliament and ANC national chairperson, Baleka Mbete, called the delayed release of results a "democratic process gone wrong." In a gathering of the Inter-Parliamentary Union, she urged representatives of 147 countries not to remain silent on the Zimbabwe issue.[65]

As ANC president, Jacob Zuma is considered the party's heir-apparent to succeed Mbeki as its presidential candidate in the country's May 2009 elections.[66] Many analysts predict that South African policy toward Zimbabwe would change under a possible Zuma administration.[67] In the meantime, public pressure may force Mbeki to take a stronger position on the growing violence in neighboring Zimbabwe: in mid-May, President Mbeki visited Zimbabwe for the second time since the elections and dispatched six retired generals to investigate reports of attacks on the opposition. The generals have reportedly expressed shock at the level of violence.[68]

A recent outbreak of xenophobic violence in South Africa has some, including ANC Treasurer Matthews Phosa, calling for early elections in South Africa.[69] In May 2008, Zimbabweans and other foreign nationals were targeted by mobs in several South African townships; at least 40 have been reportedly killed and over 25,000 have fled their homes. South Africa is home to some three to five million illegal immigrants, most from Zimbabwe, and some South Africans blame them for the country's high crime and unemployment rate and rising food prices. Mbeki and Zuma have both condemned the attacks, but the opposition has condemned the government for not addressing the tensions earlier. On May 21, Mbeki deployed the army internally for the first time since the end of apartheid to stem the violence.

The United Nations

U.N. Secretary-General Ban Ki-moon has joined the United States, Great Britain, and France in calling on the U.N. Security Council to address the Zimbabwe situation. In remarks to the Security Council on April 16, Ban expressed his deep concern with the delayed release of the electoral results, warning,

> Absent a transparent solution to this impasse, the situation could deteriorate further with serious implications for the people of Zimbabwe. The Zimbabwean authorities and the countries of the region have insisted that these matters are for the region to resolve but the international community continues to watch and wait for decisive action. The credibility of the democratic process in Africa could be at stake here.

The Secretary-General is now engaging world leaders to determine how the international community could "help the Zimbabwean people and authorities to resolve this issue."[70] His concern has been echoed by UN High Commissioner for Human Rights Louise Arbour, who said, "I am particularly concerned about reports of threats, intimidation, abuse and violence directed against NGOs, election monitors, human rights defenders and other representatives of civil society," and called on the Zimbabwean government and its security forces to "ensure the protection of all Zimbabweans, irrespective of whom they do or do not support politically."[71]

President Mbeki chaired the April 16 Security Council meeting, which was originally called by South Africa, as rotating chairman of the Council, to discuss cooperation between the United Nations and the African Union. U.S. Ambassador to the United Nations Zalmay Khalilzad recommended that a U.N.-AU mission visit the country. The only African representative to address the Zimbabwe issue at the meeting was Tanzanian President Kikwete, who praised SADC for working to "ensure that the will of the people of Zimbabwe is respected," and suggested that the regional body would meet again soon to discuss Zimbabwe.[72]

The U.N. Security Council held a special session on April 29 to discuss Zimbabwe, reportedly at the behest of incoming Security Council chair Britain. European and Latin American members pressed for a U.N. envoy to visit the country, while other delegations, including South Africa's, rejected the proposal. President Mugabe has denounced the closed session as "sinister, racist, and colonial."[73]

U.S. POLICY ON ZIMBABWE

Current U.S. Policy

Although the United States' ability to influence internal developments in Zimbabwe is limited, the U.S. government has been an outspoken critic of the Mugabe Administration. U.S. policy toward Zimbabwe has included a combination of targeted sanctions against the Government of Zimbabwe, including financial and visa sanctions against select individuals;[74] a ban on transfers of defense items and services; a suspension of non-humanitarian assistance to the government; and support for South Africa's attempt to mediate between the government and the opposition.

In reaction to the uncertainty following the March elections, the Bush Administration repeatedly called for the immediate release of the results, and in April called for all parties to accept and implement legitimate election results, "including, as appropriate, changes in the parliament, changes in the government."[75] The State Department has since expressed "deep concern" about the inadequate "chain of custody" of the ballot boxes in the weeks after the election, and has expressed its view that conditions on the ground would not currently allow for a free and fair runoff. Assistant Secretary of State Jendayi Frazer has accused Mugabe of "trying to steal the election," saying, "My preferred option would be that the will of the people be accepted. That Mr. Mugabe does the honorable thing and steps down."[76]

The Bush Administration has been highly critical of the government's role in the current wave of violence. A State Department spokesman recently urged Mugabe to "call off his dogs,"[77] and U.S. Ambassador to Zimbabwe James McGee has publicly condemned what he refers to as a "systematic campaign of violence designed to block this vote for change. ..orchestrated at the highest levels of the ruling party."[78] On May 13, Zimbabwean police tried to interfere with a multi-country diplomatic convoy outside Harare.[79] The convoy had been visiting hospitals and an alleged interrogation center, and during the encounter a policeman reportedly threatened to beat a U.S. embassy official. Ambassador McGee described seeing evidence of violence of a "massive" scope, including proof that civilians had been interrogated at "torture camp" the convoy visited.[80] He was later reportedly summoned by Zimbabwe's Foreign Minister for allegedly violating diplomatic protocol and was warned not to interfere in internal affairs. Embassy staff are collecting evidence and documenting abuses to submit to the United Nations, SADC, and the African Union.

The Administration has increased its calls for African governments to play a greater role in resolving the political impasse. During a visit by the British Prime Minister to Washington, President Bush told the media, "The United Nations and the A.U. must play an active role in resolving the situation in Zimbabwe."[81] Secretary of State Condoleezza Rice has said more bluntly, "It is time for Africa to step up."[82] Secretary Rice has engaged several SADC leaders on how to proceed, and the United States is expected to continue to press the Security Council to discuss the situation.

U.S. Assistance

The United States is one of the largest donors of humanitarian assistance to Zimbabwe, providing over $93 million in food aid in FY2007 and $55 million to date in FY2008. The Administration's FY2009 request for $45.4 million includes $19.4 million for health programs and $26 million in Economic Support Funds, much of which are designated for either governance or economic recovery efforts.[83] This reflects a substantial increase from previous years; $23.2 million was obligated in FY2007 and $22.9 million in FY2008. Democracy and governance assistance has been augmented by funding from USAID' s global Elections and Political Processes fund (EPP). These resources support political party strengthening, voter registration, and training of election monitors. According to the State Department's Congressional Budget Justification (CBJ), "in anticipation of a more moderate government arising in 2008," FY2009 funding will support programs to "re-establish and strengthen democratic institutions, processes and systems, and to build legislative consensus on democratic reform." Such programs would support legal reforms, national dialogue on key issues, civil society advocacy, and enhanced media capacity. In the event of no change in government in 2008, the CBJ proposes to reprogram these resources to aid opposition efforts to press for reforms.

Congressional Interest

Several Members of Congress have issued statements highly critical of the Mugabe Administration, the delayed release of the election results, and the ongoing political violence. Some have written letters to Bush Administration officials or African leaders. On April 25, the Senate passed S.Res. 533, introduced by Senator John Kerry, calling for the immediate release of the presidential results, an end to the political violence and intimidation, and a peaceful transition to democratic rule. The resolution also supported calls for an international arms embargo and other targeted sanctions against the Mugabe regime, and encouraged the creation of a comprehensive political and economic recovery package in the event a democratic government is installed. The House of Representatives is now considering legislation by Representative Donald Payne condemning the violence and calling for a peaceful resolution to the political crisis.

President Mugabe frequently claims that Western sanctions are to blame for the collapse of the country's economy, despite the absence of trade sanctions against Zimbabwe. In 2001, Congress passed the Zimbabwe Democracy and Economic Recovery Act (ZDERA) (P.L. 107-99), criticizing the "economic mismanagement" and "undemocratic practices" in Zimbabwe. This legislation called for consultations with allies on economic sanctions and a travel ban. It also prohibited U.S. support for financial assistance to Zimbabwe by international financial institutions until the President has been able to certify that certain conditions pertaining to the rule of law, democratic elections, and legal and transparent land reform have been met. Zimbabwe is, however, already ineligible to receive loans from the International Monetary Fund (IMF) and the World Bank's International Development Association (IDA) because it is in arrears to those institutions for debt payments.

POLICY OPTIONS[84]

Diplomatic Pressure

Human rights advocates have urged the United States and other governments to continue diplomatic calls for Zimbabwe's government to stop the violence, allow international observers for the runoff, and cease government interference with freedoms of speech and assembly. Many analysts suggest that the SADC governments may have the greatest leverage with the Mugabe Administration, but that international support for their efforts could prove helpful. The MDC and others have called for the United Nations to deploy human rights monitors to investigate the ongoing violence. Although South Africa and SADC have already deployed inquiry teams, the presence of U.N. monitors could be influential. The international community also has the option of urging the U.N. Secretary-General to appoint a special envoy to Zimbabwe, although results from the appointment of such an envoy in 2005 were limited.[85] Nevertheless, as recent developments in the region have shown, President Mugabe's allies within the international community may be less willing to publicly support his government than in the past. Some analysts have suggested that the U.S. government should take greater initiative to expose external sources of support for the government of Zimbabwe.[86]

Diplomatic efforts toward Zimbabwe may progress toward one of three possible outcomes.[87] Some have suggested that the United States, and others, should push unequivocally for Mugabe's exit, preferably through diplomacy aimed at Southern African leaders.[88] Certain senior members of ZANU-PF are reportedly amenable to negotiating a power-sharing arrangement with the MDC. According to reports, initial discussions have already begun, but have encountered stiff resistance from senior security officials (See *Accountability* below). Given observations that the current security climate will not allow for a credible runoff, a negotiated settlement may provide the most timely solution to the stalemate. However, details regarding possible immunity deals, the compliance of the security forces, and a timetable for future elections will not be easy. If talks progress, though, the United States will have to determine whether to lift of some of its targeted sanctions on select ZANU-PF members who may be invited to join a coalition government.

Recognizing that these negotiations may fail, SADC may be poised to engage the parties on steps to ensure that the runoff election meets SADC's Principles Governing Democratic Elections,[89] and that the government announces the results in a timely manner and initiates a peaceful democratic transition. Should the election fail to meet these principles, or should the security forces try prevent a democratic transition, the international community may consider tightening sanctions, declaring the Mugabe Administration illegitimate and/or recognizing Tsvangirai as President, or referring members of the regime to international justice regimes. Other options, including a possible AU suspension of the Mugabe-led government, have been discussed above (see *African Union* above).

Humanitarian Assistance

The food security situation in Zimbabwe remains critical, with an estimated 4 million people in need of food assistance in 2008. Several Southern African countries have suffered from chronic food insecurity in recent years, stemming from a combination of weather-related and man-made factors, including prolonged drought, floods, poor economic performance, and the impact of HIV/AIDS. Although drought is partly to blame for Zimbabwe's food shortages, analysts believe that disruptions to the farming sector resulting from Mugabe's land seizure program are the main reason for reduced food production.[90] Nearly all of the country's 4,500 commercial farms have now been taken by the government and redistributed or divided. The government's land redistribution program is reportedly plagued by inefficiencies, with large portions of redistributed land not being actively farmed. Tractors and other inputs to production are in short supply. Thousands of experienced farm workers were reportedly forced to flee seized commercial farms, and many of those who now hold farmland have no agricultural expertise. The displacement of farm workers and vandalism that has followed the March elections also contributes to food insecurity. The 2008 maize harvest has been severely affected by a combination of flooding followed by extreme dry weather. The crop production deficit in much of the country is estimated at 75 to 100 percent.

Global food needs have increased dramatically since the beginning of the 2008, primarily due to rising commodity and fuel prices, and the competition for international resources may severely affect the international community's ability to address food insecurity in Zimbabwe. In May 2008, the World Food Program reported a shortfall of \$272.7 million in its required resources for the country's feeding program from 2008 to 2010. Of the \$46.3 million already received from international donors, over half, \$26 million, has been provided by the United States.

Poor sanitation and water shortages pose serious health risks in Zimbabwe's urban centers. Basic hygiene items, such as soap, have become too expensive for many residents. In the country's second largest city, Bulawayo, service delivery, including garbage collection, has declined severely because of budget shortages, and reports suggest many ambulances and fire trucks sit unused because the city council cannot afford fuel or spare parts. According to U.N. reports, the current violence has impeded the delivery of assistance by NGOs.

Economic Recovery[91]

In tandem with diplomatic pressure, the Bush Administration and other international actors have discussed financial incentives and assistance to facilitate Zimbabwe's economic recovery in the event of a democratic transition. Zimbabwe's economy has collapsed in the last decade, and every sector of the economy has been affected. Annual outputs of wheat, maize, and tobacco, once Zimbabwe's largest foreign exchange earner, have plummeted. Manufacturing output dropped over 47 percent in the decade between 1996 and 2006. Zimbabwe's mining sector has been similarly affected, although the platinum industry remains a major income earner for the government.[92] World Bank and IMF lending has been suspended for more than six years due to nonpayment of arrears, and foreign currency for essential imports, particularly fuel, is in extremely short supply. Zimbabwe's inflation rate, at almost 165,000 percent according to official government figures, is the highest in the world and has contributed significantly to the country's economic collapse. Zimbabweans continue to face steep rises in the prices of food and non-food items, including rents. These factors all contribute to increasing pressure on both the people of Zimbabwe and members of Mugabe' s regime.

According to the IMF, the Reserve Bank of Zimbabwe's quasi-fiscal activities are primarily responsible for the surge in the country's money supply in recent years. Losses from such activities were estimated to be 75 percent of GDP in 2006. These activities include monetary operations to absorb excess liquidity; subsidized credit; sustained foreign exchange losses through subsidized exchange rates for selected government purchases and multiple currency practices; and financial sector restructuring. After the government implemented its price control policy in June 2007, cutting prices of basic commodities by 50 percent in an effort to stem inflation, manufacturing output fell more than 50 percent within six months and many firms were forced to close. The price controls also resulted in a shortage of basic goods and have contributed to worsening social indicators. The government's fast track land reform and more recent policy changes like the Indigenization and Economic Empowerment Act, have created significant uncertainty over property rights, deterring foreign direct investment and lowering consumer confidence.

The MDC has outlined its program to revive the economy.[93] The party has committed to stop printing new money, eliminate price controls, open foreign exchange,[94] and bring in the IMF to assist in reforming the government's fiscal policies. Tsvangirai has also floated the idea of replacing the Zimbabwe dollar with a new currency.[95] Some analysts have suggested that the existing dollar could be temporarily linked to either the South African rand or the U.S. dollar to stabilize its value. The party's economic policy stresses a free market approach, and promises to privatize most state-owned companies, dismantle patronage networks, and simplify the tax code. In recognition that the government's bloated budget has contributed significantly to current economic woes, Tsvangirai has promised a significantly smaller cabinet, should he become president, as part of a deficit-reduction strategy. In addition, the MDC has proposed a land audit and a program to "harmonize" land-tenure so that those on communal lands can hold an individual title. The party would consider compensation for those who lost land illegally.

The State Department's FY2009 budget request states that "If political change ensues and legislative restrictions are lifted, Zimbabwe will need significant support from the United States, in coordination with other donors, to reform, rebuild, and recover." Western donors, including the United States, met twice in Europe in 2007 to explore reconstruction options, and their representatives meet regularly in Harare to coordinate existing aid programs. Some reports suggest, however, that there has been little concrete planning on what this reconstruction support should entail.[96] Another donor meeting is expected in Europe in summer 2008, and a pledging conference may be considered. Norway has pledged a major economic stabilization package from Nordic countries in return for "a true democratic election" and the adoption of sound fiscal policies, although the exact amount of such a package has not been announced. Britain has made similar pledges, and maintains its willingness to release funds to pay for parts of an orderly land redistribution program if Mugabe retires and the rule of law is returned. By some estimates, the cost of Zimbabwe's economic recovery may be almost $4 billion over a five-year period to cover food support, land reform, health services and education, infrastructure, balance of payment and budget support, and emergency aid programs. In the event of political change in Zimbabwe, ESF funds in the State Department's FY2009 request would be directed toward support for "monetary and fiscal policy reform and economic revitalization, specifically agricultural and private sector productivity and improvement of the business enabling environment."

The World Bank and the IMF have developed strategies for Zimbabwe's economic recovery, but the IMF suggests that liberalizing the foreign exchange rate will require careful management. Given the need to cut government spending to reduce the government deficit, significant donor assistance will be required to rebuild the public health sector, which according to reports may have lost as much as 80 percent of its skilled workforce. Reviving the country's agriculture industry will require delicate handling to address historical grievances against white Zimbabweans regarding land distribution and tenure[97] Congress authorized $20 million in its ZDERA legislation for land reform assistance for FY2002, and some analysts suggest this level of annual assistance may still be appropriate.[98]

Accountability and Reform

The inability of the country's judicial system to protect its citizens or their property, or to provide due process to those seeking remedy or compensation, suggests a fundamental crisis in the implementation of the rule of law in Zimbabwe. Analysts suggest that the country will require significant judicial and security sector reforms as part of larger constitutional reforms. The people of Zimbabwe will also have to determine what level of accountability they may seek, not only for recent political violence, but for historical grievances and alleged official corruption under the Mugabe Administration. Tsvangirai has proposed the creation of a Truth and Reconciliation Commission similar to that of South Africa, "striking a healthy balance between reconciliation and accountability."[99] He has offered Mugabe "an honorable exit as... father of the nation," but it is unlikely that such an offer will be extended to all senior security officials implicated in acts of violence.[100] Mugabe and other senior officials, however, may resist a negotiated peaceful exit from power if they fear subsequent prosecution, as occurred with the former presidents of Liberia, Chad, and Zambia.[101]

REFERENCES

[1] The Electoral Laws Amendment Act, which came into effect on January 11, 2008, eliminated one of the two electoral administration bodies and required polling places to be located in areas readily accessible to the public. It also established a continual voter registration process and explicitly prohibited intimidation during the campaign period.

[2] See, for example, Human Rights Watch (HRW), *All Over Again: Human Rights Abuses and Flawed Electoral Conditions in Zimbabwe's Coming General Elections,* Vol. 20, No. 2(A), March 2008, and International Crisis Group (ICG), Africa Report No. 138, *Zimbabwe: Prospects from a Flawed Election*, March 20, 2008.

[3] Zimbabwe Human Rights NGO Forum, Can the Elections be Free and Fair in the Current Environment? March 18, 2008.

[4] "Opposition Party in Zimbabwe Accuses Mugabe of Printing Millions of Extra Ballots," Associated Press, March 24, 2008.

[5] Parliament passed Constitutional Amendment No. 18 in late 2007, increasing the number of parliamentary seats from 120 to 210. Following a rushed delimitation exercise, the ZEC presented its final report, which outlined changes to several constituency and ward boundaries, with no time for debate before parliament adjourned at the end of January 2008.

[6] Lance Guma, "Election Body Calls for More Polling Stations," SW Radio Africa, March 11, 2008, available at [http://www.allafrica.com].

[7] Amendments to POSA allowed groups to present notifications for rallies and demonstrations to the nearest police station, and if denied approval, provided for appeals to be dealt with in a timely manner by the local magistrates court rather than the Home Affairs Minister. Amendments to AIPPA abolished the "journalism without accreditation" offense, although journalists remain prohibited from covering official events, like elections, without accreditation. HRW, *All Over Again: Human Rights Abuses and Flawed Electoral Conditions in Zimbabwe's Coming General Elections,* Vol. 20, No. 2(A), March 2008.

[8] Zimbabwe Human Rights NGO Forum, Can the Elections in Zimbabwe be Free and Fair in the Current Environment? March 18, 2008.

[9] "Concern Over Pre-Election Environment, Election Update (1)," ZESN Press Statement, January 25, 2008.

[10] Zimbabwe Human Rights NGO Forum, Can the Elections in Zimbabwe be Free and Fair in the Current Environment? March 18, 2008.

[11] "Zimbabwe: Opposition Activists Teargassed, Beaten," *IRIN*, January 23, 2008.

[12] HRW, All Over Again: Human Rights Abuses and Flawed Electoral Conditions in Zimbabwe's Coming General Elections,Vol. 20, No. 2(A), March 2008.

[13] ICG, "Zimbabwe: Prospects from a Flawed Election," March 20, 2008.

[14] "Zim Prisons Chief Orders Officers to Vote Mugabe," Reuters, February 29, 2008.

[15] International Bar Association, Partisan Policing: An Obstacle to Human Rights and Democracy in Zimbabwe, An International Bar Association Human Rights Institute Report, October 2007.

[16] "First Poll Observers in Zimbabwe," *BBC*, March 11, 2008.

[17] "CNN Denied Permission to Cover Elections in Zimbabwe," *CNN*, March 25, 2008.

[18] Statement issued by South African Member of Parliament Diane Kohler Barnard, "DA Rejects SADC Assessment of Zimbabwe Election as 'Peaceful and Credible,'" available at [http://www.da.org.za].

[19] "Ecumenical Observers Challenge Zimbabwe Election Process and Demand Respect for the Will of the People," World Council of Churches Press Release, April 29, 2008.

[20] A *Financial Times* report suggests that ZANU-PF won ten parliamentary seats that would have been claimed by the MDC had its votes not been split between the two factions. "Acrimonious Division Cost MDC Success," *Financial Times*, April 4, 2008.

[21] The Tsvangirai faction won 99 seats and MDC-Mutambara won 10. One seat was won by an independent, and three seats remain subject to by-elections due to candidates' deaths.

[22] According to press reports, the ZEC conducted the recount in violation of a court order to stop recounts for 23 parliamentary constituencies. The MDC had petitioned the court on the basis that ZANU-PF's requests for recounts were not valid because they were not filed within 48 hours of the election in accordance with ZEC rules. The court allegedly ruled that a recount could not be ordered until after the original results were released.

[23] Makoni, 57, served as Finance Minister from 2000 to 2002 and was reportedly dismissed after criticizing the administration's economic policies.

[24] According to ZESN, Tsvangirai received 49.4% of the vote and Mugabe 41.8%."ZESN poll projections on March 29 presidential elections," ZESN press release, March 31, 2008.

[25] "Zimbabwe Opposition Strike Fails," *BBC,* April 16, 2008.

[26] "Opposition Unites Against Mugabe," *Al Jazeera,* April 28, 2008.

[27] "Crisis Looms After Harare Vote-Buying," *Financial Times*, April 11, 2008.

[28] Referring to an alleged letter between Tsvangirai and Prime Minister Gordon Brown, Zimbabwe's *Herald* accused the MDC leader of plotting "illegal regime change" and quotes outgoing Justice Minister Chinamasa , "It is clear... that Tsvangirai along with Brown are seeking regime change in Zimbabwe,and on the part of Tsvangirai, this is treasonous. ..There is no doubting the consequences for acting in a treasonous manner." The MDC

says the letter is a forgery. See "Zimbabwe Opposition Accused of Treason," *CNN*, April 17, 2008.

[29] ICG, "Negotiating Zimbabwe's Transition," *Africa Briefing No. 51*, May 21, 2008.

[30] "West Should Stop Blocking Zimbabwe's Way Forward," *The Herald* (Harare), April 23, 2008.

[31] "Rift Over Zimbabwe Unity Plan," *New York Times,* April 24, 2008.

[32] "Zimbabwe 'Too Violent for Poll,'" *BBC*, May 8, 2008.

[33] "SADC: Zim Not Yet Ready For Fair Vote," *Mail & Guardian* (Johannesburg), May 14, 2008.

[34] "Zimbabwe: Army Behind New Wave of Human Rights Abuses," HRW Press Release, April 30, 2008.

[35] As of May 9, 2008 the group reported treating 900 people. See "Mbeki Meets Mugabe for Talks," *Al Jazeera*, May 9, 2008.

[36] Statement by Ambassador James McGee, "Breaking the Silence on Political Violence in Zimbabwe," issued on May 8, 2008.

[37] Some "war veterans" have questionable credentials and some were too young to have participated in the liberation struggle. Other veterans disagree with ZANU-PF's policies.

[38] "White Former Farmers Threaten Blacks with Eviction," *The Herald*, May 7, 2008.

[39] For more information, see CRS Report RL32723, *Zimbabwe*, by Lauren Ploch.

[40] "Zimbabwe: Operation Glossary - A Guide to Zimbabwe's Internal Campaigns," *IRIN*, May 1, 2008.

[41] For further information on Operation Gukurahundi, see the report by the Catholic Commission for Justice and Peace and the Legal Resources Foundation, *Breaking the Silence - Building True Peace: A Report on the Disturbances in Matabeleland and the Midlands 1980-1988*, April 1999, available at [http://www.sokwanele.com/ pdfs/BTS.pdf].

[42] See, for example, "The Opposition Goes for Broke," *The Economist,* May 17, 2008, and "Zimbabwe Under Military Rule, Former Minister Claims," *Pretoria News*, May 12, 2008.

[43] USAID, *Zimbabwe: Complex Emergency and Drought*, Situation Report 1, May 16, 2008.

[44] "Hunger Drives Post-Election Violence, Deepens Poverty," *IRIN*, May 9, 2008.

[45] "Zimbabwe: End Violence Before June Runoff," HRW Press Release, May 16, 2008.

[46] Amnesty International, "Zimbabwe Violence Reaches Crisis Levels," May 16, 2008.
[47] "Call for State of Emergency Over Zim Violence," *Mail & Guardian*, May 14, 2008.
[48] "New Delay in Zimbabwe Elections," Voice of America, May 5, 2008.
[49] "Militias 'to Rig Zimbabwe Poll,'" *BBC*, May 9, 2008.
[50] High Court of South Africa Durban & Coast Local Division Case No. 4975/08
[51] The U.S. State Department declared the situation a "crisis" in a news briefing by State Department Spokesman Sean McCormack on April 15, 2008.
[52] Statement made during the Prime Minister's Question Time before the House of Commons, April 23, 2008, available at [http://www.number-10.gov.uk].
[53] "Zimbabwe 'A Sinking Titanic,' "*Financial Times,* March 22, 2007.
[54] SADC Communique, "2008 First Extra-ordinary SADC Summit of Heads of State and Government Issued on 13 April 2008, in Lusaka, Zambia."
[55] Fiona Forde, "Summit on Zim 'Coup' Crisis Stalls," *The Sunday Independent*, April 13, 2008.
[56] African Union Division of Communication and Information, "Communique on the Situation in Zimbabwe," April 17, 2008.
[57] Statement by the Chairman of the AU Commission on the Situation in Zimbabwe on May 6, 2008, available at [http://www.africa-union.org].
[58] "No New Poll Watchers for Zimbabwe's Runoff: State Media," *Agence France Presse*, May 17, 2008.
[59] In 2005, after the death of the President of Togo, the Togolese army installed his son as president. The AU declared the intervention to be a military coup and the AU Peace and Security Council demanded the resignation of the new president and urged members to impose diplomatic, travel, and arms sanctions until elections were held. The president stepped down the day after sanctions were imposed. It is notable, in the case of Togo, that the relevant regional body, the Economic Community of West African States (ECOWAS) played an important role in denouncing the coup and leading the campaign for sanctions. In the second instance of AU intervention, the AU suspended Mauritania from all organizational activities after the country's military led a successful coup. The president, in office for 21 years, was considered autocratic, and reports suggest that most Mauritanians supported the military's actions. Nevertheless, the AU

upheld the suspension because it opposed the unconstitutional overthrow of a civilian regime. Following an investigation, the AU decided against sanctions, but held the suspension until elections were held in 2007.

[60] Barry Bearak, "Zimbabwe Opponent Criticizes Mbeki," *New York Times*, February 14, 2008.

[61] "Zimbabwe's Political Crisis Enters South Africa Domestic Politics," Voice of America, April 17, 2008.

[62] "Zimbabwe Crisis at Critical Level, Warns Zuma," *CNN*, April 24, 2008.

[63] "Africa Shows Impatience on Zimbabwe Crisis," Reuters, April 22, 2008.

[64] "Zuma Ratchets Up Rhetoric Over Zimbabwe," *Financial Times*, April 22, 2008.

[65] Statement by Speaker Baleka Mbete in Cape Town, April 13, 2008, available at [http://www.parliament.gov.za].

[66] Zuma, who has been linked to a number of controversies, was expected to face corruption charges in August 2008, but his trial date has been postponed. If he were convicted prior to the elections, he would be ineligible to run.

[67] CRS Report RL3 1697, South Africa: Current Issues and U.S. Relations, by Lauren Ploch.

[68] "Anxiety Grows for Kidnaped Zimbabwe Activist," Voice of America, May 18, 2008.

[69] "Anti-Foreigner Violence Escalates in South Africa," Reuters, May 19, 2008.

[70] "U.N. Council and AU to debate Zimbabwe," Reuters, April 16, 2008.

[71] "Alarmed by Violence in Zimbabwe, Arbour Urges Restraint," U.N. Press Release, April 27, 2008.

[72] "Spotlight Turned on Zimbabwe at UN Council," Reuters, April 16, 2008.

[73] "Zimbabwe Dismisses U.N. Talks," Reuters, April 30, 2008.

[74] President Bush imposed these sanctions through Executive Order 13288, issued in March 2003. The Order prohibits transactions with persons, entities, or organizations found to be undermining democratic institutions and processes in Zimbabwe, who are included in a Specially Designated Nationals(SDN) list maintained by the U.S. Treasury Department's Office of Foreign Assets Control (OFAC).

[75] News Briefing by State Department Spokesman Tom Casey on April 22, 2008.

[76] News Briefing by State Department Spokesman Sean McCormack on April 15, 2008, and "Mugabe Trying to Steal Elections, Says U.S. Official," *CNN*, April 24, 2008.

[77] Daily Press Briefing by State Department Spokesman Tom Casey, May 1, 2008.

[78] Statement by Ambassador McGee, "Breaking the Silence on Political Violence in Zimbabwe," May 8, 2008, available at [http://harare.usembassy.gov].

[79] The convoy included the ambassadors of the United States, Britain, the EU, and Japan; the deputy ambassadors of Tanzania and the Netherlands; and embassy staff and journalists.

[80] "U.S. Ambassador Says Zimbabwe Government Doing Nothing to Stop Post-Election Violence," Voice of America, May 14, 2008.

[81] Remarks by President Bush during a press conference with Prime Minister Brown at the White House, April 17, 2008.

[82] On-the-Record Briefing by Secretary Rice in Washington, DC, April 17, 2008.

[83] This amount does not include food aid, which is allocated throughout the year in response to need.

[84] There have been a number of studies conducted on policy options to re-engage Zimbabwe, including, Michelle D. Gavin, *Planning for Post-Mugabe Zimbabwe,* Council on Foreign Relations (CFR) Special Report No. 31, October 2007; Todd Moss and Stewart Patrick, *The Day After Comrade Bob: Applying Post-Conflict Recovery Lessons to Zimbabwe*, Center for Global Development Working Paper no. 72, December 2005; and "After Mugabe: Applying Post-Conflict Recovery Lessons to Zimbabwe," *Africa Policy Journal*, John F. Kennedy School of Government, Harvard University, vol. 1, Spring 2006.

[85] In 2005, the Zimbabwean government implemented *Murambatsvina,* a massive demolition program aimed at allegedly illegal urban structures, which rendered over 700,000 homeless. Then-Secretary-General Kofi Annan named Tanzanian-born Anna Tibaijuka, Executive Director of UN-HABITAT, as the U.N. Special Envoy on Human Settlements Issues in Zimbabwe to investigate the humanitarian impact of the demolitions. The presentation of her report to the U.N. Security Council stirred controversy and China, Algeria, Benin, and Russia objected to debate on it. The majority of Security Council members voted to allow its discussion, albeit in a closed session. Many observers suggest the Zimbabwean government did little to respond to the U.N. envoy's recommendations.

[86] Gavin, *Planning for Post-Mugabe Zimbabwe,* CFR Special Report No. 31, October 2007.

[87] Further discussion of these outcomes may be found in ICG, "Negotiating Zimbabwe's Transition," Africa Briefing No. 51, May 21, 2008.

[88] Stephen Morrison and Mark Bellamy, "The Close of the Mugabe Era," Center for Strategic and International Studies, April 29, 2008.

[89] The 1992 Treaty establishing SADC commits member states to "consolidate, defend and maintain democracy, peace, security and stability" in the region. The Principles on Elections commits members to adhere to basic democratic standards. These principles can be found at [http://www.sadc.int/english/documents/ political_affairs/index.php].

[90] On the land takeovers in Zimbabwe, see AI, *Zimbabwe: Power and Hunger — Violations* of the Right to Food, October 15, 2004.

[91] Information in this section was drawn from a variety of sources, including David Coltart, "A Decade of Suffering in Zimbabwe: Economic Collapse and Political Repression under Robert Mugabe," *CATO Institute Development Policy Analysis No. 5*, March 24, 2008; Sonia Munoz, "Central Bank Quasi-fiscal Losses and High Inflation in Zimbabwe: A Note," *IMF Working Paper*, April 2007; and "Zimbabwe: Article IV Consultation - Staff Notes," *IMF Country Report No. 05/360*, October 2005.

[92] Zimbabwe has the world's second largest reserves of platinum, behind South Africa. The largest mining operations in the country are controlled by Impala Platinum and Anglo Platinum, respectively. These South African-owned companies are the world's largest platinum producers.

[93] See, for example, Morgan Tsvangirai, "Freedom for Zimbabwe,"*The Wall Street Journal*, March 21, 2008.

[94] The Reserve Bank made a major change to its fiscal policy in May 2008, allowing the Zimbabwe dollar to float to address hyperinflation. Analysts have expressed doubts that the government will maintain this policy if the Zim dollar depreciates faster than expected.

[95] "Tsvangirai Promises New Zimbabwe Currency," *The Australian*, March 28, 2008.

[96] Morrison and Bellamy, "The Close of the Mugabe Era," *op cit.*

[97] The U.N. Food and Agriculture Organization (FAO) has suggested that raising the yields of communal farming areas, which compose almost 50 percent of Zimbabwe's land, could guarantee its food security. The country's annual maize requirement for human consumption is estimated

at 1.4 million metric tons. The FAO estimates that a $50 million investment annually for three years to train farmers and provide seeds and fertilizer would significantly increase yields and cost less than what Zimbabwe now pays to import food. See "Zimbabwe: Small Scale Farmers Seen as Backbone of Food Security," IRIN, May 15, 2008.

[98] Gavin, *Planning for Post-Mugabe Zimbabwe,* Council on Foreign Relations Special Report No. 31, October 2007.

[99] Morgan Tsvangirai, "Freedom for Zimbabwe,"*The Wall Street Journal*, March 21, 2008.

[100] "Zimbabwe Opposition Seeks Peacekeepers for Run-off," Reuters, May 11, 2008.

[101] Former Liberian President Charles Taylor now faces war crimes charges before the Special Court for Sierra Leone at the Hague; former Chadian President Hissan Habre is expected to be tried in Senegal for human rights abuses committed by his regime; and former Zambian President Frederick Chiluba is on trial in Zambia for corruption.

In: Focus on Zimbabwe
Editor: Alfred J. Cartage, pp. 87-111
ISBN: 978-1-60692-186-9

Chapter 3

BACKGROUND NOTE: ZIMBABWE

Rainbow forms over water at Victoria Falls, Zimbabwe, March 23, 1997. [© AP Images].

PROFILE

Official Name

Republic of Zimbabwe

Geography

Area: 390,580 sq. km. (150,760 sq. mi.), slightly larger than Montana. Cities: *Capital*--Harare (pronounced Ha-RAR-e), pop. 1.5 million. *Other towns*--Bulawayo, Chitungwiza, Mutare, Gweru, Kwekwe, Masvingo, Marondera.

Terrain: Desert and savanna.

Climate: Mostly subtropical.

People

Nationality: *Noun and adjective*--Zimbabwean (sing.), Zimbabweans (pl.).

Population (2008 est.): 8 to 9 million.

Annual growth rate (2006 World Bank est.): 0.8%.

(Note: the population growth rate is depressed by an HIV/AIDS adult prevalence rate estimated to be 15.6% and a high level of net emigration.)

Ethnic groups: Shona 71%, Ndebele 16%, other African 11%, white 1%, mixed and Asian 1%.

Religions: Christianity 75%, offshoot Christian sects, animist, and Muslim.

Languages: English (official), Shona, Ndebele.

Education: *Attendance*--mandatory for primary level.

Adult literacy--90.5% (2004 est.).

Health: *Infant mortality rate*--51.7/1,000 (2006 est.).

Life expectancy--men 37 (2006), women 34 (2006).

Government

Type: Parliamentary.

Constitution: December 21, 1979.

Independence: April 18, 1980.

Branches: *Executive*--President (chief of state and head of government), Cabinet. *Legislative*--bicameral (House of Assembly and Senate). *Judicial*-- High Court, Court of Appeal, local and customary courts.

Administrative subdivisions: Town Councils and District Councils. Main political parties: Zimbabwe African National Union-Patriotic Front

(ZANU-PF); Movement for Democratic Change (MDC); United People's Party (UPP).

Economy

GDP (2007 IMF est.): U.S. $1 .437 billion.

Real GDP growth rate (2007 IMF est.): -6.1%.

Real per capita GDP: Reliable estimates of current GDP and population size are unavailable.

Avg. inflation rate: 1,694,000% year-on-year, May 2008, by official accounts; private sector estimates are roughly one and half times the official figure).

Natural resources: Deposits of more than 40 minerals including ferrochrome, gold, silver, platinum, copper, asbestos; 19 million hectares of forest (2000).

Agriculture (15% of GDP): *Types of crops and livestock*--corn, cotton, tobacco, wheat, coffee, tea, sugarcane, peanuts, cattle, sheep, goats, pigs.

Industry: manufacturing, public administration, commerce, mining, transport and communication.

Trade (2007): *U.S. exports*--U.S. $105.2 million. *U.S. imports*--U.S. $71.8 million. *Partners* (2000 est.)--South Africa 22%, U.K. 10%, Germany 9%, U.S. 8%. *Total imports* (2004)--U.S. $1 .989 billion: most of these imports were construction and agricultural machinery, transportation equipment, data processing equipment and software, industrial machinery, pharmaceuticals, fertilizers, and general manufactured products. *Major suppliers*--South Africa 34%, U.K. 10.8%, Germany 7.3%, U.S. 6%.

(Although China is now said to be the second-largest trading partner, no statistics are available.)

PEOPLE AND HISTORY

Primarily of the Bantu group of south and central Africa, the black Zimbabweans are divided into two major language groups, which are subdivided into several ethnic groups. The Mashona (Shona speakers), who constitute about 75% of the population, have lived in the area the longest and are the majority language group. The Matabele (Sindebele speakers), representing about 20% of the population and centered in the southwest around Bulawayo, arrived within the last 150 years. An offshoot of the South African Zulu group, they maintained control over the Mashona until the white occupation of Rhodesia in 1890.

More than half of white Zimbabweans, primarily of English origin, arrived in Zimbabwe after World War II. Afrikaners from South Africa and other European minorities, including Portuguese from Mozambique, also are present. Until the mid-1970s, there were about 1,000 white immigrants per year, but from 1976 to 1985 a steady emigration resulted in a loss of more than 150,000, leaving about 100,000 in 1992. Renewed white emigration in the late 1990s and early 2000s reduced the white population to less than 50,000. English, the official language, is spoken by the white population and understood, if not always used, by more than half of the black population.

Zimbabwe boasts one of Africa's highest literacy rates. Primary and secondary schools were segregated until 1979. In the first decade after independence in 1980, the educational system was systematically enlarged by the Zimbabwean Government, which was committed to providing free public education to all citizens on an equal basis. Though in the late 1970s only 50% of the black children (5-19 years old) were listed officially as attending rural schools, today most children attend primary school despite the fact that school fees are now charged for all schools at all levels. Primary through post-secondary enrollment has expanded from 1 million to about 2.9 million since independence. There is an impressive network of independent private schools and church-run mission schools that have significantly more resources and thus significantly higher school fees than government-run schools. Higher education is offered at seven state-run universities, the most prominent being the University of Zimbabwe in Harare and the National University of Science and Technology in Bulawayo, and three private church-run universities, Africa University (Methodist), Catholic University, and Solusi University (Seventh Day Adventist). There is also a large network of teacher-training, nursing, and polytechnic colleges.

Early History

Archaeologists have found Stone-Age implements and pebble tools in several areas of Zimbabwe, a suggestion of human habitation for many centuries, and the ruins of stone buildings provide evidence of early civilization. The most impressive of these sites is the "Great Zimbabwe" ruins, after which the country is named, located near Masvingo. Evidence suggests that these stone structures were built between the 9th and 13th centuries A.D. by indigenous Africans who had established trading contacts with commercial centers on Africa's southeastern coast.

In the 16th century, the Portuguese were the first Europeans to attempt colonization of south-central Africa, but the hinterland lay virtually untouched by Europeans until the arrival of explorers, missionaries, ivory hunters, and traders some 300 years later. Meanwhile, mass migrations of indigenous peoples took place. Successive waves of more highly developed Bantu peoples from equatorial regions supplanted the original inhabitants and are the ancestors of the region's Africans today.

British Settlement and Administration

In 1888, Cecil Rhodes obtained a concession for mineral rights from local chiefs. Later that year, the area that became Southern and Northern Rhodesia was proclaimed a British sphere of influence. The British South Africa Company was chartered in 1889, and the settlement of Salisbury (now Harare, the capital) was established in 1890. In 1895, the territory was formally named Rhodesia after Cecil Rhodes under the British South Africa Company's administration.

Following the abrogation of the company's charter in 1923, Southern Rhodesia's white settlements were given the choice of being incorporated into the Union of South Africa or becoming a separate entity within the British Empire. The settlers rejected incorporation, and Southern Rhodesia was formally annexed by the United Kingdom that year. Until 1980, Rhodesia was an internally self-governing colony with its own legislature, civil service, armed forces, and police. Although Rhodesia was never administered directly from London, the United Kingdom always retained the right to intervene in the affairs of the colony, particularly in matters affecting Africans.

After 1923, European immigrants concentrated on developing Rhodesia's rich mineral resources and agricultural potential. The settlers' demand for more land led in 1934 to the passage of the first of a series of land apportionment acts that reserved certain areas for Europeans.

In September 1953, Southern Rhodesia was joined in a multiracial Central African Federation with the British protectorate of Northern Rhodesia and Nyasaland in an effort to pool resources and markets. Although the federation flourished economically, the African population, who feared they would not be able to achieve self-government with the federal structure dominated by White Southern Rhodesians, opposed it. The federation was dissolved at the end of 1963 after much crisis and turmoil, and Northern Rhodesia and Nyasaland became the independent states of Zambia and Malawi in 1964.

Unilateral Declaration of Independence (UDI)

The European electorate in Rhodesia, however, showed little willingness to accede to African demands for increased political participation and progressively replaced more moderate party leaders. In April 1964, Prime Minister Winston Field, accused of not moving rapidly enough to obtain independence from the United Kingdom, was replaced by his deputy, Ian Smith. Prime Minster Smith led his Rhodesian Front Party to an overwhelming victory in the 1965 elections, winning all 50 of the first roll seats and demoralizing the more moderate European opposition.

Although prepared to grant independence to Rhodesia, the United Kingdom insisted that the authorities at Salisbury first demonstrate their intention to move toward eventual majority rule. Desiring to keep their dominant position, the white Rhodesians refused to give such assurances. On November 11, 1965, after lengthy and unsuccessful negotiations with the British Government, Prime Minister Smith issued a Unilateral Declaration of Independence (UDI) from the United Kingdom.

Post-UDI Events

The British Government considered the UDI unconstitutional and illegal but made clear that it would not use force to oppose it. On November 12, 1965, the United Nations also determined the Rhodesian Government and UDI to be illegal and called on member states to refrain from assisting or recognizing the Smith regime. The British Government imposed sanctions on Rhodesia and requested other nations to do the same.

On December 16, 1966, the UN Security Council, for the first time in history, imposed mandatory economic sanctions on a state. Rhodesia's primary exports including ferrochrome and tobacco, were placed on the selective sanctions list, as were shipments of arms, aircraft, motor vehicles, petroleum, and petroleum products to Rhodesia. On May 29, 1968, the Security Council unanimously voted to broaden the sanctions by imposing an almost total embargo on all trade with, investments in, or transfers of funds to Rhodesia and imposed restrictions on air transport to the territory.

In the early 1970s, informal attempts at settlement were renewed between the United Kingdom and the Rhodesian administration. Following the April 1974 coup in Portugal and the resulting shifts of power in Mozambique and Angola, pressure on the Smith regime to negotiate a peaceful settlement increased. In addition, sporadic antigovernment guerilla activity, which began in the late 1960s, increased dramatically after 1972, causing destruction, economic dislocation, casualties, and a slump in white morale. In 1974, the major African nationalists groups--the Zimbabwe African Peoples Union (ZAPU) and the

Zimbabwe African National Union (ZANU), which split away from ZAPU in 1963--were united into the "Patriotic Front" and combined their military forces, at least nominally.

In 1976, because of a combination of embargo-related economic hardships, the pressure of guerilla activity, independence and majority rule in the neighboring former Portuguese territories, and a U.K.-U.S. diplomatic initiative, the Smith government agreed in principle to majority rule and to a meeting in Geneva with black nationalist leaders to negotiate a final settlement of the conflict. Blacks represented at the Geneva meeting included ZAPU leader Joshua Nkomo, ZANU leader Robert Mugabe, United African National Council (UANC) chairman bishop Abel Muzorewa, and former ZANU leader Rev. Nadabaningi Sithole. The meeting failed to find a basis for agreement because of Smith's inflexibility and the inability of the black leaders to form a common political front.

On September 1, 1977 a detailed Anglo-American plan was put forward with proposals for majority rule, neutrally administered with pre-independence elections, a democratic constitution and the formation of an integrated army. Reactions were mixed, but no party rejected them. In the interim, on March 3, 1978, the Smith administration signed the "internal settlement" agreement in Salisbury with Bishop Muzorewa, Rev. Sithole, and Chief Jeremiah Chirau. The agreement provided for qualified majority rule and elections with universal suffrage. Following elections in April 1979, in which his UANC party won a majority, Bishop Muzorewa assumed office on June 1, becoming "Zimbabwe-Rhodesia's" first black prime minister. However, the installation of the new black majority government did not end the guerilla conflict that had claimed more than 20,000 lives since 1972.

Shortly after British Prime Minister Margaret Thatcher's conservative government took power in May 1979, the British began a new round of consultations that culminated in an agreement among the Commonwealth countries as the basis for fresh negotiations among the parties and the British involving a new constitution, free elections, and independence.

The British and the African parties began deliberations on a Rhodesian settlement at Lancaster House in London on September 10, 1979. On December 10, 1979, in preparation for the transition under British authority to officially recognized independence, the "Zimbabwe-Rhodesia" reverted de facto to colonial status. On December 12, British Governor Lord Christopher Soames arrived in Salisbury to reassert British authority over the colony. His arrival signaled the end of the Rhodesian rebellion and the "internal settlement," as well as the beginning of Zimbabwe's transition to independence. The United

Kingdom lifted all remaining sanctions against Zimbabwe that day. The United States lifted sanctions effective December 16.

On December 21, after 3 months of hard bargaining, the parties signed an agreement at Lancaster House calling for a ceasefire, new elections, a transition period under British rule, and a new constitution implementing majority rule while protecting minority rights. The agreement specified that upon the granting of independence, the country's name would be Zimbabwe. The same day, the UN Security Council endorsed the settlement agreement and formally voted unanimously to call on member nations to remove sanctions.

During the transition period, nine political parties campaigned for the February 27-29 pre-independence elections. The elections were supervised by the British Government and monitored by hundreds of observers, most of whom concluded that, under the prevailing circumstances, the elections were free and fair and reflected the will of the people. Robert Mugabe's ZANU (PF) party won an absolute majority and was asked to form Zimbabwe's first government.

In a series of public statements during the transition period, Prime Minister Mugabe indicated that he was committed to a process of national reconciliation and reconstruction as well as moderate socioeconomic change. His priorities were to integrate the various armed forces, reestablish social services and education in rural areas, and resettle the estimated one million refugees and displaced persons. Mugabe also announced that his government would begin investigating ways of reversing past discriminatory policies in land distribution, education, employment, and wages.

Mugabe stated that Zimbabwe would follow a nonaligned foreign policy and would pursue a pragmatic relationship with South Africa. He noted that while Zimbabwe opposed apartheid and would support democratic change in South Africa, it would not provide bases for anti-South African guerillas.

The British Government formally granted independence to Zimbabwe on April 18, 1980. Most nations recognized Zimbabwe following independence. The United States was the first nation to open an embassy in Salisbury (Harare) on that day. Parliament convened for the first time on May 13, 1980. Zimbabwe became a member of the United Nations on August 25, 1980.

In seeking national reconciliation, Prime Minister Mugabe's first cabinet comprised members of ZANU-PF, PF-ZAPU, and independent white members of parliament (MPs) and senators. The government embarked on an ambitious reconstruction and development program and instituted increases in minimum wages. Land redistribution proceeded under four experimental models on land that the government had purchased at market rates from willing sellers.

Zimbabwe Since Independence

Prime Minister Mugabe's policy of reconciliation was generally successful during the country's first two years of independence, as the former political and military opponents began to work together. Although additional blacks were hired to fill new places in the civil service, there was no retribution for those whites who had worked for the Smith regime. Smith and many of his associates held seats in the parliament where they participated freely in debates. Likewise, Joshua Nkomo, Mugabe's rival as leader of the nationalist forces, was included in the first cabinet along with several other members of PF-ZAPU.

Splits soon developed, however. In 1981, several MPs from Smith's party left to sit as "independents," signifying that they did not automatically accept his anti-government posture. More importantly, government security officials discovered large caches of arms and ammunition on properties owned by ZAPU, and Nkomo and his followers were accused of plotting to overthrow Mugabe's government. Nkomo and his closest aides were expelled from the cabinet.

As a result of what they perceived as persecution of Nkomo (known as "Father Zimbabwe") and of his party, PF-ZAPU supporters, some of them deserters from the army, began a loosely organized and ill-defined campaign of dissidence against the government. Centering primarily in Matabeleland, home of the Ndebeles who were PF-ZAPU's main followers, this dissidence continued through 1987 and involved attacks on government personnel and installations, armed banditry aimed at disrupting security and economic life in the rural areas, and harassment of ZANU-PF members. Occasionally, some demanded that Nkomo and his colleagues be reinstated in the cabinet. More frequently, however, dissidents called for the return of farms and other properties seized from PF-ZAPU.

Because of the unsettled security situation immediately after independence and the continuing anti-government dissidence, the government kept in force a "state of emergency," which was first declared before UDI. This gave government authorities widespread powers under the "Law and Order Maintenance Act," including the right to detain persons without charge.

In 1983-84, the government declared a curfew in areas of Matabeleland and sent in the army in an attempt to suppress dissidents. Credible reports surfaced of widespread violence and disregard for human rights by the security forces during these operations, and the level of political tension rose in the country as a result. The pacification campaign, known as the "Gukuruhundi," or strong wind, resulted in as many as 20,000 civilian deaths. Nkomo and his lieutenants repeatedly denied any connection with the dissidents and called for an all-party conference to discuss the political problems facing the country. In the 1985 elections, ZANU-PF increased its majority, holding 67 of the 100 seats. ZANU-PF and PF-ZAPU agreed to unite in December 1987, and the parties formally merged in December 1989.

In October 1987, in accordance with the Lancaster House Accords, the constitution was amended to end the separate roll for white voters and to replace the whites whose reserved seats had been abolished; among the new members were 15 whites in the Senate and House of Assembly. Elections in March 1990 resulted in another overwhelming victory for Mugabe and his party, which won 117 of the 120 election seats. However, voter turnout was only 54%, and the campaign was not free and fair although the actual balloting was. Not satisfied with a de facto one-party state, Mugabe called on the ZANU-PF Central Committee to support the creation of a de jure one-party state in September 1990 and lost. The state of emergency was lifted in July 1990.

After the remaining restrictions of the Lancaster House agreement expired on April 18, 1990, the government embarked on a campaign of amending the existing constitution. Both the judiciary and human rights advocates fiercely criticized some of the first amendments, which were enacted in April 1991, because they restored corporal and capital punishment and denied recourse to the courts in cases of compulsory purchase of land by the government.

During the 1990s students, trade unionists and workers often demonstrated to express their discontent with the government. Students protested in October 1990 against proposals for an increase in government control of universities and again in May 1991 and May 1992, when they clashed with police. Trade unionists and workers were also vocal critics of the government during this time. In June 1992, police prevented trade unionists from holding anti-government demonstrations. In 1994, there was widespread industrial unrest. In August and September 1996, thousands of civil servants demanding salary increases organized a national strike and in October and November of the same year, nurses and junior doctors went on strike over salary issues. On November 14, 1997, about 50,000 war veterans demanded and received compensation equivalent to about U.S. $1,300 per person for their war service. This immense and unbudgeted expenditure created a huge fiscal deficit. The Zimbabwe dollar lost more than half its value on that day, and the Zimbabwe Stock Exchange collapsed. This event marked the beginning of Zimbabwe's ongoing macro-economic crisis.

In part through its control of the media, the huge parastatal sector of the economy, and the security forces, the government managed to keep organized political opposition to a minimum through most of the 1990s. Beginning in 1999, however, Zimbabwe experienced a period of considerable political and economic upheaval. Opposition to President Mugabe and the ZANU-PF government had grown, in part due to worsening economic and human rights conditions. The opposition was led by the Movement for Democratic Change (MDC), which was established in September 1999.

The MDC's first opportunity to test opposition to the Mugabe government came in February 2000, when a referendum was held on a draft constitution proposed by the government. Among its elements, the new constitution would have permitted President Mugabe to seek two additional terms in office, granted government officials immunity from prosecution, and authorized government seizure of white-owned land. The referendum was handily defeated. Shortly thereafter, the government, through a loosely organized group of war veterans, sanctioned an aggressive land redistribution program often characterized by forced expulsion of white farmers and violence against both farmers and farm employees.

Parliamentary elections held in June 2000 were marred by localized violence, and claims of electoral irregularities and government intimidation of opposition supporters. Nonetheless, the MDC succeeded in capturing 57 of 120 seats in the National Assembly.

The March 2002 presidential election was preceded by months of intensive violence and intimidation against MDC supporters, and more than 50 people, mostly opposition supporters, were killed. President Mugabe was declared the winner over challenger Morgan Tsvangirai by a 56% to 42% margin. Most international observers condemned the election as seriously flawed--the preelection environment was neither free nor fair, and the election itself was marred by significant fraud and rigging--but regional opinions were mixed. Soon after the election, the MDC filed a petition challenging Mugabe's victory, citing flaws in electoral laws, electoral irregularities and pre-election violence. As of the end of 2004, the case had not yet been decided.

As a result of the 2002 election, the United States, the EU, and other European countries imposed travel restrictions against senior Zimbabwean officials and embargoed the sale of arms to Zimbabwe. The U.S. and the EU also froze the financial assets of selected ruling party officials. The Commonwealth suspended Zimbabwe from council meetings for one year after its election observer team found the election neither free nor fair. At the mid-term suspension review in March 2003, the three-country committee charged with deciding Zimbabwe's fate decided to continue the suspension until the next Commonwealth meeting in December 2003. At this meeting, despite vigorous campaigning by South Africa, Zimbabwe was not invited to attend the meeting and the Commonwealth decided to continue with the suspension. Immediately after this, Mugabe withdrew Zimbabwe from the Commonwealth.

Following the 2002 presidential election, the political climate remained tense and intensely polarized. Violence escalated in the run up to rural council elections in September 2002 and various parliamentary by-elections that year. Parliamentary by-elections in Kuwadzana, Highfield, Zengeza, and Lupane in 2003 were marred by widespread intimidation and beatings. The government also passed legislation that curtailed free speech, free press, and rights of assembly. In March 2003, MDC leaders Morgan Tsvangirai, Welshman Ncube, and Renson Gasela went on trial for treason. Charges against Ncube and Gasela were subsequently dropped and in October 2004 Tsvangirai was found not guilty. In August 2005, the government dropped a second charge of treason against Tsvangirai.

The government subscribed to the electoral principles of the Southern African Development Community (SADC) in 2004 but failed to implement key elements of the principles in advance of the 2005 parliamentary elections. The campaign period and election day were largely non-violent, but the elections were not free and fair. The election process was marred by repressive legislation that limits freedom of speech and assembly; millions of expatriate Zimbabweans were not permitted to vote; the government used food distributions to influence an increasingly hungry population; an astonishingly high 10% (as high as 30% in some areas) of would-be voters were turned away; and discrepancies in officially announced results and the government's refusal to release key voting data led to questions about the possibility of fraud.

In May 2005, the government began Operation Murambatsvina (also known as Operation Restore Order), ostensibly to rid urban areas of illegal structures, illegal business enterprises, and criminal activities. A UN Special Envoy sent to Zimbabwe to assess the scope and impact of operation estimated that some 700,000 people nationwide lost their homes, their source of livelihood, or both. Families and traders, especially at the beginning of the operation, were often given no notice before police destroyed their homes and businesses. Others were able to salvage some possessions and building materials but often had nowhere to go, despite the government's statement that people should be returning to their rural homes. Thousands of families were left unprotected in the open in the middle of Zimbabwe's winter. The government interfered with non-governmental organization (NGO) efforts to provide emergency assistance to the displaced in many instances. Some families were removed to transit camps, where they had no shelter or cooking facilities and minimal food, supplies, and sanitary facilities. The operation continued into July 2005, when the government began a program to provide housing for the newly displaced. As of September 2007, housing construction fell far short of demand, and there were reports that beneficiaries were mostly civil servants and ruling party loyalists, not those displaced. The government campaign of forced evictions continued in 2006, 2007, and 2008 albeit on a lesser scale.

In April 2007, South African President Thabo Mbeki, at the behest of SADC and the international community, was designated to serve as mediator between Robert Mugabe's government and the MDC. The mediation aimed to define a mutually agreed upon election date and procedures to rewrite the constitution. While the mediations were ongoing, Mugabe announced that "harmonized" elections would be held on March 29, 2008, despite Morgan Tsvangirai's protests that the mediation was still underway and that there was not enough time to campaign. As in 2005, the pre-election period was not free and fair. The environment was characterized by violence and a media environment that heavily favored Mugabe. Although Tsvangirai was allowed to campaign, Zimbabwean police did not grant permission to MDC to hold all of its rallies, and some MDC activists were intimidated and beaten in the weeks before the election. Foreign journalists were not granted permission to cover the story from Zimbabwe. Election day was largely peaceful, with international observers from the African Union, SADC, and the Pan African Parliament present; observers from Western nations, including the United States, were not invited.

The "harmonized" elections for the presidency, House of Assembly, Senate, and local government demonstrated a significant shift in the political environment. MDC secured a majority in the parliament, giving the MDC control of the legislative branch. In the presidential race, MDC's Tsvangirai secured 47.9%, while Mugabe came in second with 43.2%. Simba Makoni, who left Mugabe's ZANU-PF party in February 2008 to run as an independent, received 8.3%. The results in the presidential race were not released until May 2, 2008. This lengthy delay called into question the credibility and independence of the Zimbabwe Electoral Commission (ZEC). Initially the MDC challenged the results, asserting that Tsvangirai had secured the majority of votes needed to win the presidency. Because no candidate secured the 50%-plus-one needed, a runoff was set for June 27, 2008.

As of early June 2008, over 50 Zimbabweans had been killed, at least 2,000 injured, and over 30,000 displaced as a result of widespread post-election violence, including state-sponsored violence. Due to these and other events, and out of concern for the lives of his MDC supporters, Tsvangirai announced in late June that he would not contest the runoff election. Voters went to the polls on June 27, and Mugabe was inaugurated for a new term as president on June 29.

FOREIGN RELATIONS

Since independence, Zimbabwe has enunciated and follows a policy of "active nonalignment." In practice, this has meant that Zimbabwe usually adhered to positions established by the Non-Aligned Movement (NAM); the Organization of African Unity (OAU), now the African Union; or, until it withdrew in 2003, the Commonwealth. Zimbabwe took a particular interest in the search for independence for Namibia (South-West Africa) from South Africa. In addition, as chairman of the front-line states in southern Africa, Zimbabwe spoke out vigorously against the policies of apartheid in South African and frequently called for the imposition of economic sanctions against Pretoria. In November 1982, Zimbabwe was chosen by the OAU to hold one of the non-permanent seats in the UN Security Council for the following two years, which brought it onto the center stage of world events and gave it much-needed experience in international affairs. In 1986, Zimbabwe was the site of the NAM summit meeting; Prime Minister Mugabe became chairman of that organization, giving both Mugabe and Zimbabwe added international visibility and responsibility.

Zimbabwe maintains embassies in the Angola, Australia, Austria, Belgium, Botswana, Canada, China, Cuba, Democratic Republic of the Congo, Egypt, Ethiopia, France, Germany, Ghana, India, Iran, Italy, Japan, Kenya, Kuwait, Malawi, Malaysia, Mozambique, Namibia, Nigeria, Russia, South Africa, Sweden, Switzerland, Tanzania, United Kingdom, the United States, Serbia, Zambia, Indonesia, Brazil, and Libya. Fifty-three countries are represented in Harare, as are several international organizations including UN institutions, the European Union, and the World Bank. Zimbabwe is a member of many international organizations, including the International Monetary Fund (IMF); African Development Bank; The World Trade Organization; Southern African Development Community (SADC); Preferential Trade Area for Eastern and Southern Africa (PTA); African Caribbean and Pacific Countries (ACP, in association with the EU); Group of 77 (G-77); Group of 15 (G-15); NAM; African Union (AU); Customs Cooperation Council (CCC); and the World Federation of Trade Unions. Shortly after the March 2002 presidential election, the Commonwealth suspended Zimbabwe from leadership councils for one year after the Commonwealth's election observer team found the conduct of the election seriously flawed. After this suspension was upheld in December 2003, Mugabe withdrew Zimbabwe from the Commonwealth. The IMF closed its Zimbabwe office in October 2004.

Historically, Zimbabwe's closest links have been with the U.K.; however, in the past eight years, this relationship has been very strained. The government has demonized Britain in the press, blaming the country for Zimbabwe's problems, and claiming that Britain reneged on promises made at Lancaster House to provide money for land reform. As with the U.S., thousands of Zimbabweans studied in the U.K., and private links remain close; however, official relations are strained.

Other West European countries have ties with Zimbabwe. The Scandinavian countries share certain philosophical affinities and have provided much assistance, as have France, Canada, and the Federal Republic of Germany. Portugal and Greece maintain links partly because of the sizable Portuguese and Greek communities in the country. Similar historical ties have led to the establishment of relations with India and Pakistan, and to a lesser extent, with Bangladesh. The government's "Look East" policy has led to closer diplomatic relations with East Asian countries such as Malaysia and China.

Zimbabwe maintains diplomatic relations with virtually every African country, although some ties are closer than others. African nations with embassies in Harare are Algeria, Angola, Botswana, D.R.C., Egypt, Ethiopia, Ghana, Kenya, Libya, Malawi, Mozambique, Namibia, Nigeria, South Africa, Sudan, Tanzania, and Zambia.

Zimbabwe developed and maintains close ties with a number of revolutionary states and organizations. Among these are the People's Republic of China, Cuba, the Democratic People's Republic of Korea, Iran, Libya, and the Palestine Liberation Organization.

GOVERNMENT

According to Zimbabwe's constitution, the president is head of state and head of government, and is elected by popular majority vote. Parliament is bicameral and sits for up to a 5-year term. On October 1, 2007 Constitutional Amendment 18, which provides for significant changes in the country's electoral dispensation, went into effect. The amendment set out the framework to harmonize presidential and parliamentary elections, to reduce the presidential term of office from 6 years to 5, to increase the number of seats in the House of Assembly and in the Senate, to empower parliament to serve as an electoral college should the office of president become vacant for any reason, and to empower the Zimbabwe Electoral Commission (ZEC) to delimit parliamentary and local constituencies. The 210-member House of Assembly is entirely elected by voters in 210 constituencies. Sixty of the 93 Senators are directly elected by voters. Other Senators include 10 provincial governors and 5 others that are appointed by the president, 16 chiefs that are elected by other chiefs, plus the president and deputy president of the Council of Chiefs.

The Zimbabwean constitution institutionalizes majority rule and protection of minority rights. The elected government controls senior appointments in the public service, including the military and police, and the independent Public Service Commission is charged with making appointments at lower levels on an equitable basis.

The judiciary is headed by the chief justice of the Supreme Court who, like the other justices, is appointed by the president on the advice of the Judicial Service Commission. The constitution has a bill of rights containing extensive protection of human rights. The bill of rights could not be amended for the first 10 years of independence except by unanimous vote of the parliament.

Zimbabwe is divided into ten provinces, each administered by a provincial governor appointed by the president. The provincial administrator and representatives of several service ministries assist the provincial governor.

Principal Government Officials

President--Robert Mugabe

Vice Presidents--Joseph Msika and Joice Mujuru

Foreign Minister--Simbarashe Mumbengegwi

Ambassador to the U.S.--Machinvenyika Tobias Mapuranga

Zimbabwe maintains an embassy in the United States at 1608 New Hampshire Ave., NW, Washington, DC 20009 (tel. 202-332-7100). A Zimbabwean mission to the United Nations is located at 19 East 47th St., New York, NY.

ECONOMY

Properly managed, Zimbabwe's wide range of resources should enable it to support sustained economic growth. The country has an important percentage of the world's known reserves of metallurgical-grade chromite. Other commercial mineral deposits include coal, platinum, asbestos, copper, nickel, gold, and iron ore. However, for the country to benefit from these mineral deposits, it must attract foreign direct investment.

In the early 1970s, the economy experienced a modest boom. Real per capita earnings for blacks and whites reached record highs, although the disparity in incomes between blacks and whites remained, with blacks earning only about one-tenth as much as whites. After 1975, however, Rhodesia's economy was undermined by the cumulative effects of sanctions, declining earnings from commodity exports, worsening guerilla conflict, and increasing white emigration. When Mozambique severed economic ties, the Smith regime was forced to depend on South Africa for access to the outside world. Real gross domestic product (GDP) declined between 1974 and 1979. An increasing proportion of the national budget (an estimated 30%-40% per year) was allocated to defense, and a large budget deficit raised the public debt burden substantially.

Following the Lancaster House settlement in December 1979, Zimbabwe enjoyed a brisk economic recovery. Zimbabwe inherited one of the strongest and most complete industrial infrastructures in sub-Saharan Africa, as well as rich mineral resources and a strong agricultural base. Real growth for 1980-81 exceeded 20%. However, depressed foreign demand for the country's mineral exports and the onset of a drought cut sharply into the growth rate in 1982, 1983, and 1984. In 1985, the economy rebounded strongly due to a 30% jump in agricultural production. However it slumped in 1986 to a zero growth rate and registered a 3% contraction in GDP in 1987 due primarily to drought and a foreign exchange crisis. Growth in 1988-90 averaged about 4.5%.

Since the mid-1990s, this infrastructure has been deteriorating rapidly, but remains better than that of most African countries. Poor management of the economy and political turmoil have led to considerable economic hardships. The Government of Zimbabwe's chaotic land reform program, recurrent interference with the judiciary, and maintenance of unrealistic price controls and exchange rates have led to a sharp drop in investor confidence. Since 1999, the national economy has contracted by as much as 40%; inflation vaulted over 1,000,000% (year on year) in May 2008; and there have been persistent shortages of foreign exchange, fuel, and food. Direct foreign investment has all but evaporated. In a desperate attempt to control inflation, the government forced firms and supermarkets to reduce prices by half in July 2007, which resulted in severe shortages of basic and other commodities.

Agriculture is no longer the backbone of the Zimbabwean economy. Large-scale commercial farming has been effectively destroyed over the course of the last eight years under the government's controversial land reform efforts starting in 2000. Corn is the largest food crop and tobacco had traditionally been the largest export crop, followed by cotton. Tobacco production in 2006, however, slumped to its lowest level--about 50 million kg--since independence, off from a peak in 2000 of 237 million kg, before recovering to 73 million kg in 2007. Gold production, another former key foreign currency source, was less than one-third of its 1999 level in 2007. Poor government management has exacerbated meager corn harvests in years of drought or floods, resulting in significant food shortfalls every year since 2001.

Paved roads link the major urban and industrial centers, but the condition of urban roads and the unpaved rural road network has deteriorated significantly since 1995 for lack of maintenance. Rail lines connect with an extensive central African railroad network, although railway track condition has also worsened in recent years, along with locomotive availability and utilization. The electric power supply has become erratic and blackouts are common due to unreliable or nonexistent coal supplies to the country's large thermal plants and power plant breakdowns. Telephone service is problematic, and new lines are difficult of obtain. Municipal water supply is also erratic.

The largest industries are metal products, food processing, chemicals, textiles, clothing, furniture and plastic goods. Most manufacturers have sharply scaled back operations due to the poor operating climate and foreign exchange shortages. Zimbabwe is not eligible for preferred trade status under the African Growth and Opportunity Act (AGOA). Zimbabwean producers still export lumber products, certain textiles, chrome alloys, and automobile windscreens to the U.S.

Zimbabwe is endowed with rich mineral resources. Exports of gold, asbestos, chrome, coal, platinum, nickel, and copper could lead to an economic recovery one day. No commercial deposits of petroleum have been discovered, although the country is richly endowed with coal-bed methane gas that has yet to be exploited.

With international attractions such as Victoria Falls, the Great Zimbabwe stone ruins, Lake Kariba, and extensive wildlife, tourism historically has been a significant segment of the economy and contributor of foreign exchange. The sector has contracted sharply since 1999, however, due to the country's declining international image.

Energy Resources

With considerable hydroelectric power potential and plentiful coal deposits for thermal power station, Zimbabwe is less dependent on oil as an energy source than most other comparably industrialized countries, but it still imports 40% of its electric power needs from surrounding countries--primarily Mozambique. Only about 15% of Zimbabwe's total energy consumption is accounted for by oil, all of which is imported. Zimbabwe imports about 1.2 billion liters of oil per year. Zimbabwe also has substantial coal reserves that are utilized for power generation, and coal-bed methane deposits recently discovered in Matabeleland province are greater than any known natural gas field in Southern or Eastern Africa. In recent years, poor economic management and low foreign currency reserves have led to serious fuel shortages.

DEFENSE

At independence, then-Prime Minister Mugabe declared integrating Zimbabwe's then three armed forces as one of his government's top priorities. A unified army was created by combining the Zimbabwe African National Liberation Army (ZANLA), the Zimbabwe Peoples' Revolutionary Army (ZIPRA), and the Rhodesian Security Forces (RSF). In July 1994, the combined Zimbabwe Defense Forces (ZDF) Headquarters was created. Currently the armed forces of Zimbabwe are completely integrated and are composed of an army (ZNA) and an air force (AFZ).

The Zimbabwe Defense Forces (ZDF) is under the command of the president, who is the commander-in-chief of the Defense Forces. He is assisted by the Minister of Defense, who is responsible for the administrative and logistical support of the Defense Forces, and the commander of the Defense Forces, who maintains operational control of the Defense Forces. Subordinate to the commander of the Defense Forces are the commander of the Zimbabwe National Army (ZNA) and the commander of the Air Force of Zimbabwe (AFZ).

The ZNA is authorized 40,000 members but endstrength estimates as of June 2008 indicated the ZNA had about 30,000 members serving. The ZNA's operational forces are based in Harare, Bulawayo, Masvingo, and Mutare. Operational forces include five infantry brigades, artillery brigade, mechanized brigade, field artillery regiment, engineer regiment, air defense regiment, commando regiment, and one airborne battalion. Today, the ZNA is beset by shortages of supplies, including food. It is mostly under-trained and its equipment is aged, not particularly reliable, and largely immobile.

The AFZ is authorized 5,000 members, but only 4,000 were on active duty as of June 2008. It is estimated that half of Zimbabwe's aircraft are mission capable.

The Zimbabwe Republic Police numbers 25,000. The force is organized by province, and is comprised of uniformed national police, the Criminal Investigation Department, and traffic police. It also includes specialized support units including the (paramilitary) Police Support Unit and riot police and a Police Internal Security and Intelligence unit. The police commissioner- general exercises overall command of the force.

The U.S. Congress terminated support for military cooperation programs in 2001. Presently, the U.S. has no military-to-military cooperation with Zimbabwe other than through the President's Emergency Plan for AIDS Relief (PEPFAR) program.

U.S.-Zimbabwean Relations

After the Unilateral Declaration of Independence in November 1965, the United States recalled its Consul General from Salisbury, closed the U.S. Information Service (USIS) library, and withdrew its Agency for International Development (USAID) and trade promotion officials. After 1965, the small remaining American consular staff continued to operate under authority of exequaturs issued by Queen Elizabeth II. Following declaration of a republic, the United States closed its Consulate General on March 17, 1970.

In 1971, despite Administration opposition, the U.S. Congress passed legislation permitting the United States to import strategic materials, such as chrome, from Rhodesia. The legislation, which took effect January 1, 1972, was of little real economic benefit to the Rhodesian economy, and the United States continued to support the balance of the sanctions program. After the legislation was repealed in March 1977, the United States once again enforced all sanctions.

The United States supported the United Nations and the United Kingdom consistently in their efforts to influence Rhodesian authorities to accept the principles of majority rule. Beginning in 1976, the United States began to take a more active role in the search for a settlement in cooperation with the British. The Anglo-American proposals of late 1977, aimed at bringing a negotiated end to the dispute, lent the weight of the United States to the search for a peaceful settlement and were a counterpart to the Soviet-Cuban use of military power to increase their influence in southern Africa. The United States supported British efforts to bring about and implement the settlement signed at Lancaster House on December 21, 1979 and extended official diplomatic recognition to the new government immediately after independence. A resident Embassy was established in Harare on Zimbabwe's Independence Day, April 18, 1980. The first U.S. Ambassador arrived and presented his credentials in June 1980. Until the arrival in 1983 of a resident Ambassador in Washington, Zimbabwe's relations with the U.S. were handled by its Ambassador to the United Nations (UN) in New York.

At the Zimbabwe conference on reconstruction and development (ZIMCORD) in March 1981, the United States pledged $225 million over a 3-year period toward the government's goals of postwar reconstruction, distribution and development of land, and the development of skilled manpower. By the end of FY 1986, the United States had contributed $380 million, the majority in grants, with some loans and loan guarantees. However, in July 1986, the U.S. Government decided to discontinue future bilateral aid to Zimbabwe as a result of a continuing pattern of uncivil and undiplomatic statements and actions by the Government of Zimbabwe in the United Nations and elsewhere. Aid programs previously agreed upon were not affected by the decision, nor were regional development programs that might benefit Zimbabwe. Full programming was restored in 1988.

USAID assistance to Zimbabwe since 2002 has focused on family planning, HIV/AIDS prevention, democracy and governance programs, emergency food aid, and assistance to internally displaced persons. The Centers for Disease Control and Prevention (CDC) began a direct assistance program in August 2000. CDC's program consists of prevention of HIV transmission; improved care of persons with HIV/AIDS; surveillance, monitoring, and evaluation of the epidemic; and health sector infrastructure support.

Since 2000, the United States has taken a leading role in condemning the Zimbabwean Government's increasing assault on human rights and the rule of law, and has joined much of the world community in calling for the Government of Zimbabwe to embrace a peaceful democratic evolution. In 2002 and 2003, the United States imposed targeted measures on the Government of Zimbabwe, including financial and visa sanctions against selected individuals, a ban on transfers of defense items and services, and a suspension of non-humanitarian government-to-government assistance. Despite strained political relations, the United States continues as a leading provider of humanitarian assistance to the people of Zimbabwe, providing about $400 million in humanitarian assistance from 2002-2007, most of which was food aid.

President Mugabe visited Washington informally in September 1980, and on official working visits in September 1983, July 1991, and in 1995, meeting with Presidents Carter, Reagan, Bush, and Clinton respectively. He has also led the Zimbabwean delegation to the UN on several occasions, including most recently in 2007. Vice President George Bush visited Harare in November 1982 on a trip to several African countries.

Principal U.S. Officials

Ambassador--James D. McGee

Deputy Chief of Mission--Katherine Dhanani USAID Mission Director--Karen Freeman Political/Economic Chief--Glenn Warren Public Affairs Officer--Paul Engelstad Defense Attaché--LTC Ryan McMullen

Offices of the U.S. Mission

U.S. Embassy (Chancery)

172 Herbert Chitepo Avenue, Harare Tel: 263-4-250-593

Fax: 263-4-796-488

U.S. Agency for International Development 1 Pascoe Avenue Belgravia, Harare Tel: 263-4-252-401 Fax: 263-4-252-478

Public Affairs Section 7th Floor, Gold Bridge Eastgate, Harare

Tel: 263-4-758-800

TRAVEL AND BUSINESS INFORMATION

The U.S. Department of State's Consular Information Program advises Americans traveling and residing abroad through Country Specific Information, Travel Alerts, and Travel Warnings. Country Specific Information exists for all countries and includes information on entry and exit requirements, currency regulations, health conditions, safety and security, crime, political disturbances, and the addresses of the U.S. embassies and consulates abroad. Travel Alerts are issued to disseminate information quickly about terrorist threats and other relatively short-term conditions overseas that pose significant risks to the security of American travelers. Travel Warnings are issued when the State Department recommends that Americans avoid travel to a certain country because the situation is dangerous or unstable.

For the latest security information, Americans living and traveling abroad should regularly monitor the Department's Bureau of Consular Affairs Internet web site at http://www.travel.state.gov, where the current Worldwide Caution, Travel Alerts, and Travel Warnings can be found. Consular Affairs Publications, which contain information on obtaining passports and planning a safe trip abroad, are also available at http://www.travel.state.gov. For additional information on international travel, see http://www.usa.gov/Citizen/ Topics/ Travel/ International.shtml.

The Department of State encourages all U.S citizens traveling or residing abroad to register via the State Department's travel registration website or at the nearest U.S. embassy or consulate abroad. Registration will make your presence and whereabouts known in case it is necessary to contact you in an emergency and will enable you to receive up-to-date information on security conditions.

Emergency information concerning Americans traveling abroad may be obtained by calling 1-888-407-4747 toll free in the U.S. and Canada or the regular toll line 1-202-501-4444 for callers outside the U.S. and Canada.

The National Passport Information Center (N PIC) is the U.S. Department of State's single, centralized public contact center for U.S. passport information. Telephone: 1-877-4USA-PPT (1-877-487-2778). Customer service representatives and operators for TDD/TTY are available Monday-Friday, 7:00 a.m. to 12:00 midnight, Eastern Time, excluding federal holidays.

Travelers can check the latest health information with the U.S. Centers for Disease Control and Prevention in Atlanta, Georgia. A hotline at 877-FYI-TRIP (877-394-8747) and a web site at http://wwwn.cdc.gov/travel/default.aspx give the most recent health advisories, immunization recommendations or requirements, and advice on food and drinking water safety for regions and countries. A booklet entitled "Health Information for International Travel" (HHS publication number CDC-95-8280) is available from the U.S. Government Printing Office, Washington, DC 20402, tel. (202) 512-1800.

Further Electronic Information

Department of State Web Site. Available on the Internet at http://www.state.gov, the Department of State web site provides timely, global access to official U.S. foreign policy information, including Background Notes and daily press briefings along with the directory of key officers of Foreign Service posts and more. The Overseas Security Advisory Council (OSAC) provides security information and regional news that impact U.S. companies working abroad through its website http://www.osac.gov

Export.gov provides a portal to all export-related assistance and market information offered by the federal government and provides trade leads, free export counseling, help with the export process, and more.

STAT-USA/Internet, a service of the U.S. Department of Commerce, provides authoritative economic, business, and international trade information from the Federal government. The site includes current and historical trade-related releases, international market research, trade opportunities, and country analysis and provides access to the National Trade Data Bank.

INDEX

B

C

D

E

F

G

Q

R

S

T

U

V

W

Z